The Life and Times of

GEORGE PENROSE WOOLLCOMBE

Educator

Vic Rivers '58
My old schoolmate
and friend
Stephen Woollcombe

Written By

Stephen Woollcombe

The image on the front cover is of the G. P. Woollcombe memorial window in the Ashbury College chapel. It symbolizes his life and work, the three large panels representing him as a teacher, as spiritual leader and as counsellor.

 FriesenPress

Suite 300 - 990 Fort St
Victoria, BC, V8V 3K2
Canada

www.friesenpress.com

ISBN
978-1-4602-8902-0 (Hardcover)
978-1-4602-8903-7 (Paperback)
978-1-4602-8904-4 (eBook)

1. BIOGRAPHY & AUTOBIOGRAPHY, EDUCATORS

Distributed to the trade by The Ingram Book Company

Table of Contents

Foreword. v

Preface. ix

Prologue xiii

I. In the beginning… 1

   Genesis 1
   Ancestors and siblings of GPW 5
   Family life in Loudwater 6
   Royal Grammar School 8

II. University Years 13

   George "goes up" to Oxford 13
   What Oxford gave him 19

III. Early Years in Canada 23

   Crossing the Atlantic 23
   Beginning to teach 25
   1891 – "Mr. Woollcombe's School" is born 27
   Wedding bells 34
   His brothers' keeper 38
   Ashbury House School 41
   At home with Julia 44
   Tragedy! 48

IV. The Argyle Years – Evolution and Growth. 53

   The new century 53
   Jessie to the rescue 54
   His persona evolves 57
   A busy summer 59
   The Ashbury College Company Limited 61
   Settling into Argyle 63

Family life in Argyle 65

His philosophy of education 67

Becoming Reverend 71

The Lennoxville connection 74

Grave temptation 75

V. Rockcliffe 81

The big move 81

Social networks 86

Life and work in Rockcliffe 88

A day in the life of the headmaster 89

Jessie, his closest partner 91

The schoolmaster 96

The Englishman 103

GPW and the Board 111

The Empire, the King, the Bible, and Christian morality 116

Sunny years at Ashbury 121

Slowing down 128

Saying farewell 130

VI. The Last Chapters of his Life 135

Back to his roots 135

Adventure at sea 144

His last years 151

Descendants of G.P. Woollcombe 165

Epilogue 167

Afterword 169

Acknowledgements and Sources 171

About The Author 177

Foreword

by Andrew Cohen

Canada is often called a "young country", a statutory declaration much favoured by breathless politicians on Canada Day. As a functioning democracy, though, Canada is relatively old among the nations of the world. Few countries have had its continuity and stability.

In fundamental ways Canada – dear, dull, durable Canada – looks much like it did at Confederation in 1867. Institutionally, the federal system of government, the power of the provinces, the commitment to democracy and the free market are much the same.

In other ways, though, we remain a young society. Unlike the Europeans, we do not have institutions – cultural, educational, political – going back centuries. We do not have ancient libraries, fortresses and churches. Indeed, even as we approach our 150th anniversary, much of what we have built in Canada is less than a century old. Heritage means something different in the new world than in the old.

All of that makes Ashbury College special. As it celebrates the 125th anniversary of its founding, we realize just how unusual it is. While there are schools in Canada older than Ashbury, it is among the best and most venerable.

So let us say this: In enduring as long as it has, with the distinction it has, with the values it has, with the teachers and students it has, Ashbury College is a national institution. As Canadians, we are often reluctant to see this or say it of our schools, but age – with its accumulated wisdom – does matter, particularly in a country a century and half old.

But how did Ashbury come to be? Did it arrive fully formed and fully clothed, falling from the Heavens onto the grassy fields of Rockcliffe Park? Why is it in the national capital? Why has it survived and succeeded?

The answer is George Penrose Woollcombe, the founder of Ashbury and its first headmaster. Woollcombe is intimately and inextricably associated with Ashbury. Without his vision, there would be no Ashbury College – or at least not the Ashbury we know today.

In the history of Ashbury, Woollcombe is the indispensable man. He imagined Ashbury, built Ashbury, filled Ashbury, ran Ashbury. He did this, prudently and diligently, for 42 years. It was a remarkable run. No head of school since has stayed as long or done as much. For a generation, we might say, Woollcombe *was* Ashbury.

Stephen Woollcombe, a graduate of the school, tells the extraordinary story of his grandfather with sensitivity and candour. In a sense, his biography of George Woollcombe is a biography of the school – engaging, illuminating and important.

This was a long, full, feverish life. Woollcombe was born in 1867, just six weeks before Confederation. He founded the school in 1891 and retired in 1933, months after Adolf Hitler and Franklin Roosevelt came to power. He died in 1951.

His life spanned the last third of the nineteenth century and the first half of the twentieth. Much happened. He saw the Boer War and the Korean War and two world wars in between. He watched Queen Victoria and the Empire yield to King George VI and the Commonwealth. He saw prime ministers from Sir John A. Macdonald to Louis St. Laurent, and many governors-general, whom he came to know well as neighbours and friends.

As his grandson writes, the life of George Woollcombe was ambitious. Degree from Oxford in hand, steeped in the lessons of the Church, he left England for Canada. It was no small thing. He taught in different schools in different places, seeking something more challenging, before coming to Ottawa.

He had the idea of a boy's school, teaching values – English school values – and he brought it to fruition. Over the years, he established it and expanded it and nurtured it.

Life was not always easy; he knew grievous personal loss and the school did not always meet his expectations, particularly in his remuneration. But he weathered the crisis of war, depression and changing standards over the decades.

He built a reputable school, attracting fine teachers, graduating good students. Many thrived in science, business, the law, medicine and politics at home and abroad. He made a difference.

All along, he hewed to his morality, rooted in his fervent Christianity. Today the school is no longer all white, male and Christian. Its students are of both sexes, of many races and religions. They and Ashbury's teachers come from everywhere, speaking a variety of tongues.

And while the curriculum has changed, the campus is bigger and enrolment is larger, at the core the education remains about excellence, effort, independence, growth and compassion.

Ashbury College is more diverse and more egalitarian. But what matters still, as Woollcombe always said, is "to serve others, to do your best."

Andrew Cohen is a journalist, author and professor of journalism and international affairs at Carleton University. His son Alexander and daughter Rachel are graduates of Ashbury.

Preface

Initially the motivation for writing this book came to me as I delved into my family's background. It is not uncommon for people to become interested in their own genealogy as they get older. Young people generally don't have the time.

As a boy growing up in Ottawa, I became particularly aware of my father's family: my Woollcombe uncles and aunts and cousins, my Granny, who died when I was eight, and especially my Granddad. He lived until I was twelve. I remember my parents always referred to him with respect and affection. Frequently, I would visit him at his home a block down the street. Sometimes on Sundays, I would go with my parents and sister for the mid-day meal. Other times I would go alone with my cocker spaniel, who would gallop up the staircase ahead of me to the old man's study. My dog would be welcomed with half an arrowroot biscuit, a chuckle, and pats on the head. Granddad would always then sit me down and inquire in detail about my schooling. He would sometimes give me a book to read. Once on my birthday, he gave me a Bible, another time *The Book of Common Prayer*. In the summer, he would visit us at our cottage at Meech Lake. On December 25th in the evening, he would come to our house to preside quietly, more by his presence than by his words, over Christmas dinner with the family. Near the end of the festivities, we would watch him sip his single glass of brandy and smoke his one cigarette.

These early family memories of G. P. Woollcombe were reinforced by the aura surrounding his name at Ashbury College. That is where I took my primary and secondary schooling. We boys understood from the adults around us that he was the living embodiment of the school's history. Although he had retired as headmaster a quarter century previously, the character of Ashbury had not changed greatly from his day. Often "the Founder" would be seen visiting the school for events such as football games or special chapel services. His dress was old-fashioned.

He was small of stature and walked with a cane, but he always captured our attention. Once a year he would address the assembled students, telling stories from the past and inevitably some words about desirable values and behaviour. Then he would request that the boys be granted a "half-holiday", at which we would cheer.

Over the years since then, my image of this man has evolved. I became curious to place him in a historical context. Since his time, so much has fundamentally changed in Canada, in Ottawa and at Ashbury – socially, politically and economically. My own career as a diplomat and a teacher, combined with my continuing association with Ashbury and my family background, gave me grounds to ask questions about George Penrose Woollcombe. As I examined more closely his life and work I was increasingly conscious of his virtues and achievements along with his evident foibles and contradictions.

One aspect that struck me was how his English roots were central to his whole narrative: He was an Englishman – born, bred and educated in Victorian England. However, he made his life's work in a Canada that was just emerging from its colonial roots. In this sense, this story is as much a reflection of Canada as it is about him.

An equally central and continuous theme of the story was his driving, lifetime commitment to educating young people. Here we must bear in mind that this was an era when the methods and values of Canadian education were very different from today. We also need to understand that everything in Woollcombe's life was governed by his faith in God, – a perception more difficult to comprehend in modern Canadian society, where current attitudes about religion are drastically different from those days.

In these ways the study of G. P. Woollcombe's life has offered me insight into the historical base of our present society.

If one were to boil down into a few words Woollcombe's most essential core human values, those which his whole life as an educator was dedicated to passing on, and on which ultimately he should be judged, these must be: serve others, and do your best. Service – and striving for excellence.

This biography is a labour of love – and of curiosity. However, I have been greatly helped by the substantial support of Ashbury College, whose archives I have scoured and, most critically, which has provided the necessary financial commitment with my publisher, FriesenPress. The book is published this year in the context of Ashbury's 125th anniversary, commemorating the school's founding by G. P. Woollcombe in 1891. Needless to say, the content and conclusions are entirely my own, quite independent of Ashbury.

Over the past several years I have systematically spoken, again and again, with all living members of Woollcombe's family, as well as with every person I could reach who had any memories of him, even second-hand recollections. In the same way, I have amassed many personal letters and scores of old photographs and documents. Of course, the Internet has been a constant and major source of my research findings. A number of friends and relatives have read over and commented usefully on the manuscript at various stages. A detailed account of all my sources and acknowledgments is provided at the end of the book.

A final small note about style: The subject of this biography is referred to in many ways – 'G. P. Woollcombe', 'Woollcombe', 'the headmaster', 'the Head', 'G.P.', 'Dr. Woollcombe', 'George', etc. In each case this choice of name is deliberate and relates to what I consider appropriate for the particular context at hand. Also, for simplicity's sake I have often found it convenient here and there to simply use 'GPW' as his designation.

Stephen Woollcombe
Ottawa, June 2016

Prologue

On June 14th, 1933, in an emotional leave-taking ceremony on the sunny lawn of Ashbury College, an old man, slight of stature but of commanding presence, wearing a dark suit, clerical collar, academic gown with its scarlet and white hood, formally addressed the assembled students, teachers and dignitaries:

> *...It is now almost forty-two years since I founded the school, which is therefore in a very special sense my "child"...*

> *...As I look back over the past, I am only too conscious that I have made many a mistake and in the words so well known to us "I have left undone those things that I ought to have done". But I can honestly say that I have tried to help and to develop along right lines every boy whom I have been privileged to have in my care; and I think I can venture to say that in the great majority of cases the boys themselves have realized and appreciated my efforts for their welfare. It is necessarily a great and severe wrench for me to relinquish my post here and to say goodbye to Ashbury, but I have decided that it is best for me to do so. ... Wherever I may be, Ashbury will always have first place in my affections.*

Several decades later some of GPW's former pupils offered their assessment of him:

- *Taught responsibility. Outstanding character builder. Backbone of Ashbury.*

- *Very stern, very fair. Gentle father figure especially for the younger boys. Poised. Unflappable.*

- *Dr. Woollcombe WAS Ashbury! It was his creation, was shaped by him and reflected this long after he had retired. Although he liked to appear as a stern authoritarian, he was kindly, had real understanding of boys and an interest in individuals. In my case, and I believe it to be true of staff and students, he was respected and regarded with great affection. When he preceded a caning with "This hurts me more than it does you", one could believe it. He invariably concluded such sessions with "Go and sin no more, my son."*

– *He had incredible energy and the quick darting movements of a bird. In fact, he resembled an emaciated eagle with a bald head and a scrawny neck encased in a Roman collar several sizes too large.*

I. In the beginning...

Genesis

On Sunday May 21st, 1867, George Penrose Woollcombe was born in a country vicarage in the village of Loudwater in Buckinghamshire, England. His parents were Henrietta Woollcombe (née Jacob) and the Reverend William Penrose Woollcombe. They had been married five years, Henrietta had already given birth to three girls and was nearly thirty years old. This was their first son, and they were full of joy. The couple would not stop there however, but went on to beget four more sons, as well as four more daughters. Quite consciously they were following the stern scriptural injunction to "be fruitful and multiply". When her nearly annual child-bearing duty came to an end Henrietta was 43.

William Penrose was from a long line of Woollcombe scholars and clergymen. Before him, both his father and his grandfather had been Oxford graduates of classical studies and Church of England clerics, as indeed were several great-uncles, uncles, brothers, and a brother-in-law. Others were officers in the Royal Navy. Henrietta's family had a similar heritage over several generations, including her father, the Reverend George Andrew Jacob, D.D., a noted classical scholar and headmaster of the distinguished church-related school, Christ's Hospital in London. Their newborn son George was to become steeped in the tradition of both his parents.

Reinforcing this sense of heritage was the Woollcombe genealogical line, which could be traced back ten generations to the year 1497. They had been landed gentry in the county of Devon, southwest England. For most of these centuries, the seat of William Penrose's branch of the family was a manor house called Ashbury. The Woollcombe name had always been and still is closely associated with the Ashbury name and with Devonshire, even though William Penrose's grandfather was the last in the line to have been born in Ashbury House, in 1754. The family that George was born into no longer owned land or an estate. They were respected as clerics and scholars and were well established, but far from wealthy or commercially successful. Nor were they nobility. In class-conscious 19th century England, all this was formative in shaping the social values and ethos of George's upbringing.

Ashbury House in Devonshire

This was the Woollcombe family's ancestral manor house.

William Penrose Woollcombe was born in 1827 in another Devonshire town, Ilsington, where his father, Rev. William Woollcombe also was vicar. Unlike his own children, William Penrose had to get along with only four siblings! After graduating from Christ Church, Oxford, he took holy orders to be deacon in 1851 and priest in 1852. (Half a century later his son George would follow the same sequence.) In 1862, at age 34, he married Henrietta, who was 24.

The formal recommendation for his appointment as Vicar of

Loudwater in 1865 (having served two years as assistant curate) gives some insight into W. P. Woollcombe's character. The principal trustee at the time, arguing in his favour, stated, "...I cannot desire to see a very high churchman at Loudwater, and I am sure such a man would not succeed. I am very anxious that a man should go there of piety and activity, a gentleman and a thorough, hearty Churchman, and if possible, a man of property... I know of a man who fulfills every one of these qualifications."

These qualities in his father set the tone of young George's upbringing. There were other aspects of his father's character, as we will see, that may also have influenced him, both positively and negatively.

Loudwater at that time was an essentially self-contained rustic community of 700 souls situated in a pretty, winding valley on the road between Oxford and London. The journey to the outskirts of London took a couple of hours by coach. By the rail line, which had been constructed about ten years previously, the trip took only an hour. However, it is unlikely that many of the villagers had strayed that far from home in their whole lives. The main economic activity in the village and surroundings was farming, but there were also a number of paper mills.

And so William and Henrietta moved into the Vicarage and stayed there for the next 34 years, raising their large family and tending to several generations of the parish flock. When, in failing health, the old vicar retired in 1897, his devoted parishioners provided him with a beautifully inscribed testimonial scroll stating:

> "...We cannot allow you to retire from our midst without an expression of our sincere sympathy with you and your family, and also the high respect and esteem which we entertain for you both as regards your Christian character, and the services you have so faithfully rendered to the parish for so long a time..."

They added to this a sum of money to help the couple out "in the evening of your life". William then moved with Henrietta to the seaside resort of Ramsgate in Kent. He died there in 1899, and she the next year.

William Penrose Woollcombe, Vicar of Loudwater. GPW's father.

Henrietta Woollcombe, née Jacob. GPW's mother.

Ancestors and siblings of GPW

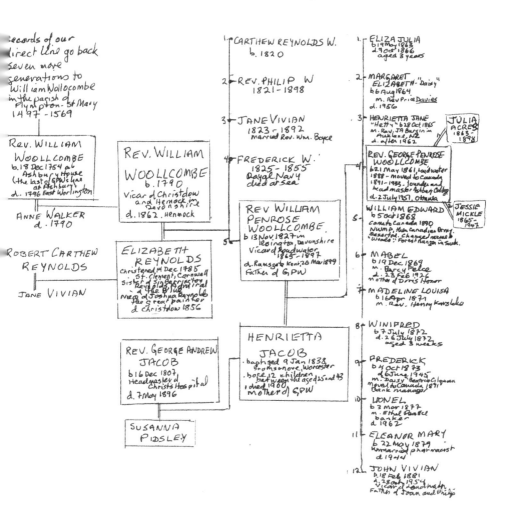

Records of our direct line go back seven more generations to William Woollocombe in the parish of Plympton-St Mary 1497-1569

Rev. WILLIAM WOOLLCOMBE
b.18 Dec 1754 at Ashbury House (the last of GPW's line at Ashbury) d. 1796 East Worlington

ANNE WALKER d. 1790

ROBERT CARTHEW REYNOLDS

JANE VIVIAN

REV. WILLIAM WOOLLCOMBE
b. 1790
Vicar of Christow and Hennock in Devonshire
d. 1862. Hennock

ELIZABETH REYNOLDS
Christened 14 Dec 1785
St. Clement, Cornwall
Sister of Sir Frederick Pollard Admiral of the Blight
Niece of Joshua Reynolds the great painter
d. Christow 1856

REV. GEORGE ANDREW JACOB
b 16 Dec 1807
Headmaster of Christs Hospital
d. 7 May 1896

SUSANNA PIDSLEY

1. CARTHEW REYNOLDS W. b. 1820

2. REV. PHILIP W 1821-1898

3. JANE VIVIAN 1823-1892 married Rev. Wm. Boyce

4. FREDERICK W. 1825-1855 Royal Navy died at sea

REV WILLIAM PENROSE WOOLLCOMBE
b 13 Nov 1827 m Ilsington, Devonshire
Vicar of Loudwater 1865-1897
d. Ramsgate Kent, 28 May 1899
Father of GPW

HENRIETTA JACOB
baptised 9 Jan 1838 Bromsenove, Worcester
bore 12 children best between the ages 25 and 43
died 1900
mother of GPW

1. ELIZA JULIA b 19 May 1863 d. 9 Oct 1866 aged 3 years

2. MARGARET ELIZABETH "Daisy" b 6 Aug 1864 m. Rev Price Davies d. 1956

3. HENRIETTA JANE "Hetty" b 28 Oct 1865 m. Rev. JA Burgin in Auckland, NZ d. after 1962

JULIA ACRES 1863 - 1898

REV. GEORGE PENROSE WOOLLCOMBE
b 21 May 1861, Loudwater 1888 - moved to Canada 1891-1935 - founder and headmaster Ashbury College
d. 2 July 1957, Ottawa

WILLIAM EDWARD
b 5 Oct 1868
Came to Canada 1890
NWMP, then Canadian Army deserted. Changed name to "Woods". Forest Ranger in Sask.

JESSIE MICKLE 1865-1947

6. MABEL b 19 Dec 1869 m. Barry Felce d. 23 Feb 1926 mother of Dris Honor

7. MADELINE LOUISA b 16 Apr 1871 m. Rev. Henry Kawsleko

8. WINIFRED b 7 July 1872 d. 26 July 1872 aged 3 weeks

9. FREDERICK b 4 Oct 1873 d 6 June 1945 m. Daisy Beatrice Gilpin moved to Canada 1871 bank manager

10. LIONEL b 3 Mar 1877 m. Ethel Campbell banker d 1962

11. ELEANOR MARY b 22 May 1879 unmarried pharmacist d 1944

12. JOHN VIVIAN b 18 Feb 1881 d. 28 Oct 1954 Vicar of Loudwater Father of Joan and Philip

Family life in Loudwater

The physical world that baby George entered, the Vicarage, was a three-storey red-brick house. It was relatively substantial, in keeping with the social importance of the Vicar's position in the village community in those times. The house, at that time, adjoined the church building, and the door from the Vicar's study actually opened into the family pew in the church. The newborn's crib was in the upstairs nursery, shared with his elder sisters Daisy, aged three, and Hettie, one and a half. The first-born child, Eliza, had died at age 3½. Mortality in very young children was common in those days. William and Henrietta's bedroom was nearby. Downstairs were the kitchen, the dining room, the parlour, and the Vicar's study.

The Vicarage, in Loudwater, where GPW grew up.

The three live-in servants were all local women from neighbouring villages: the cook, a mature woman, who later had her own baby boy while living there; a scullery maid who assisted the cook; and the nursery maid, helping Henrietta with the children. The latter two servants were girls in their teens. Their rooms were in the attic.

The house, which belonged to the church, was typical of the times for a middle-class professional family in a rural setting. There was no electricity: oil lamps were used. Nor, of course, was there central heating: the large coke-burning stove in the kitchen offered heat in the winter, and there was a log-burning fireplace in the parlour. At night everyone was equipped with earthenware hot-water bottles filled with boiling water to warm their beds before they slept. Water was drawn by a hand pump from a well on the property. The only tap was in the kitchen. There were weekly baths in the big, circular zinc tub for the children, sometimes three or four at a time, usually Saturday evening. Food was preserved in a cold-stone larder, and there may also have been an icebox with blocks of ice insulated by sawdust. There was no sewage system and the large house had one outside toilet for that whole large family plus the servants, so as many as fifteen people used it. It was called "the earth closet" and was regularly emptied of its contents, which were then carefully spread as fertilizer on the kitchen garden.

Several years later, when George was sixteen and had been joined by eight more siblings, the parish built a new, more spacious vicarage for the family. It was similarly equipped but no longer attached to the church and had a surrounding garden. As explained in an early historical account, "In 1883, the Ecclesiastical Commissioners granted £1,500 towards defraying the cost of a new vicarage." The old building, erected ninety years earlier, was pulled down. The new one, still standing, can be visited today on Google Earth and seen essentially as it was then. Such an unbelievable fantasy would have been beyond the old Vicar's comprehension!

As George was growing up, life revolved around the church. This directly and indirectly infused all family activity and conversation.

Prayers at meals and at bedtime were a constant, natural part of George's daily life and remained so until he died. Everything during the week was affected by, or completely determined by church-related activities: Father's preparation of his sermon, religious education of the children by their parents, and so on. There were frequent and natural demands by parishioners on both the Vicar and his wife; Henrietta would often need to be there to offer solace or support, especially to the women and children. On Sunday morning the whole family would file from their home into their special pew in the church for the service.

The Vicar's sermons were famous for their length, as well as their fastidious exposition of Christian moral values. At one point he was asked discreetly to keep an hourglass visible on his pulpit railing as a silent check on his verbosity. Wicked tongues used to chatter about the church sexton and how he would hide some liquid refreshment behind one of the gravestones across the road to sustain him so he could quietly escape during the long sermons.

Family life for young George was not totally restricted to Loudwater and surroundings. There would occasionally be picnic excursions, and visits to relatives, notably the Jacobs, his mother's family, with whom the Woollcombes always remained closely in touch. The Jacobs also often made reciprocal visits to Loudwater. The family usually had summer holidays on the seacoast at Ramsgate, and occasionally at Clacton in Essex. On these holidays, their time was spent mainly reading, boating, and just resting.

Royal Grammar School

As their children approached the age to enter school, William and Henrietta considered where they should be sent. William, something of an autocrat and without doubt a moralist, was opposed to "Public Schools" such as Eton or Harrow, proclaiming them full of lazy, rich, and immoral young men. Even sodomy was suspected. William was making a virtue of necessity, since he couldn't afford to send his sons there. In any event, there happened to be an excellent grammar school conveniently close by. Just three miles down the country road in the village of High Wycombe was the Royal Grammar School (RGS), so the choice became obvious. The girls on the other hand were sent to a boarding school in Brighton, Sussex. Later, the younger children, Eleanor and John, were also taught by their elder sisters, Daisy and Hettie. However, the older girls were resented by their young siblings who considered them too strict!

Thus, when he was seven years old George started at RGS. This school would become an important determinant in his approach to education. This is where he received all his primary and secondary schooling. By the mid-19th century most of England's old, established Public Schools and grammar schools had undergone basic reform, featuring rigorous discipline, master-approved values, and common features such as team games, prefects and division of students into 'houses'. The impressions and values, the habits and the practices instilled in George at RGS would give him the model he was later to adopt as headmaster of Ashbury College.

The Royal Grammar School was founded in the middle of the 16th century and received a royal charter from Queen Elizabeth I in 1562. Lacking a strong endowment, over the centuries it had to struggle for local financial support. It nonetheless continued to offer a classical curriculum for boys and also provided almshouses for local poor people. By the time George entered RGS, it had seen an upsurge in support and had strengthened both its educational mission as well as its charitable work. In 1852 the trustees raised the headmaster's annual salary to a respectable £50 and hired the curate of High Wycombe, Rev. James Poulter, as Head. Rev. Poulter and his successor, G.J. Peachell would have a formative influence on young George. Poulter strengthened the school's academic excellence, continuing the classical emphasis. Under him an efficient school had started to emerge. He made a point of personally teaching classes, a practice later followed by George throughout his years as Ashbury's head. He also instituted external examinations of boys' progress. Sports, and in particular cricket, were promoted as an important part of school life. George, who had a small but wiry, muscular frame, excelled in cricket and in track-and-field.

Royal Grammar School, circa 1880, in the village of High Wycombe, near Loudwater. This is where GPW received all his primary and secondary schooling, from 1873 to 1885.

Under Mr. Peachell a new school building was built behind the ancient structure – which was largely demolished. The school was not large in those years, with an enrolment of less than 100 boys, about four fifths being day-boys. Subsequently, throughout the 20th Century, the RGS enrolment as well as the scope of its curriculum, expanded greatly. By 1963 there were about one thousand boys in the school. In some respects, the comparison of the Royal Grammar School with Ashbury College is striking.

George was followed at RGS by all his brothers in turn: first Willy, then Fred, then Lionel and finally John. All but John, who was aged four when George graduated from the school, were there at the same time.

John`s son Philip Woollcombe, who is still alive, recounts the family lore about all four older boys heading off together to school each morning, three miles down the road to High Wycombe. Only George, being the eldest, was privileged to have a bicycle. Their father maintained he could only afford one. It was an old-fashioned "penny-farthing". The others walked.

GPW, aged about 17, sporting his new moustache.

The Vicar would often complain that his stipend was low and there were no other substantial sources of income. Behind his back the children would refer to him ironically as the "the poor vicar", or sometimes, in view of his autocratic bent, as "the Governor". To his face, of course, he was always respectfully just called "Father". More endearingly and without irony, Mother was referred to as "the precious queen".

II. University Years

George "goes up" to Oxford

George benefitted from his senior status among his siblings in other respects, notably by further education. He was the only son the Vicar felt he could afford to send to university. Later on, brothers Willy, Fred and Lionel, as we shall see, quickly followed George to Canada, shipped off by their father without university education. The youngest son, John did end up going to Cambridge, but he paid his own way, after his parents had died, thanks to his inheritance. As for George's sisters, in the 1880s higher education was generally still not available to middle-class daughters who were usually tutored at home. Except for Eleanor, who took technical training as a pharmacist and never married, the girls all became housewives and moved away from Loudwater.

In George's case, the Vicar made a written contract with him to pay for his Oxford education in the amount of £150 per annum up to a total of £500. George formally agreed that it would be deducted from his ultimate inheritance. His father, being conscientiously fair to all his children, stipulated that this amount should be added to George's sisters' inheritance. Reflecting the close control the Vicar exercised over his children, he doled the money out to George over the three years only in small amounts as needed for particular purposes on a case-by-case basis. This contract and George's detailed accounting to his father of the sums he received were found among his papers when he died, along with his father's long, handwritten last will and testament.

There was never any question as to where specifically George should go to study. It would certainly be Oxford, seen as the apex of higher learning in England – and some would say, in the whole world. Conveniently Oxford was located only a few miles away from Loudwater. Moreover, of all the 36 constituent colleges comprising the university, it was clear that George should attend Christ Church. This prestigious college was oriented to serve particularly both ecclesiastical and aristocratic families. The Vicar himself had graduated from Christ Church some four decades previously. Tradition and William Penrose Woollcombe's paternal ambition demanded it be thus.

GPW, in his first year at Oxford.

Accordingly, on May 26th, 1885, five days after his eighteenth birthday, George took the short train journey to Oxford to secure admission, called 'Matriculation', to Christ Church. This was a matter of no great difficulty. He was armed with a good record at Royal Grammar School, he was the first son of a respectable Church of England family and his father had likely paved the way with a letter of reference to the Dean. One month later, the time-honoured Oxford process required George to sit for an oral exam, called "Responsions", with a panel of tutors who reviewed what he had learned at RGS, essentially in Greek, Latin, and Maths. They also discussed and advised him on his future course of studies. Finally, on October 16th, George "went up" (another Oxford expression) to reside in Christ Church and begin his studies.

**'The Hall' at Christ Church, Oxford. This is where
GPW always dined while at Oxford.**

Christ Church was founded by Cardinal Wolsey in 1525 in the reign of Henry VIII. It boasted impressively august classical buildings and surrounding grounds, which are largely the same today as in

Woollcombe's time. In fact much of Evelyn Waugh's popular novel and the later TV drama, *Brideshead Revisited*, were set in Christ Church, as were the movies of J.K.Rowling's *Harry Potter* series. So George would have had his evening meal in the same great gothic dining room used by the wizardry students at Hogwarts! It was called simply "The Hall". The students wore academic gowns and grace was intoned in Latin.

Some forty years later, Waugh's shiftless roué in *Brideshead*, Sebastian, lived in the same residence as George did, the Meadow Building. This elegant four-storey Venetian-style structure had been recently built in the 1860s. George's room probably looked southwards to the River Thames across the landscaped Christ Church Meadow. He and his fellow students would take time out to stroll along the landscaped pathways, while chatting, or silently, peacefully contemplating.

These were mainly happy times for him, not least because they were his first sustained period away from the constraints of his Loudwater home life and the discipline of school. Apart from his studies, he engaged in those college sports available to undergraduates at that time such as cricket, and possibly boating but not likely foxhunting which was the leisure pastime of the wealthy and aristocratic. He may well have been active in the debating club. Later in life, as headmaster of Ashbury College he personally encouraged and led school debates. He certainly socialized cheerfully with other serious young gentlemen.

However surprising it might sound to modern minds, as he was "coming of age", between the 18 and 21 years old, he had practically no sustained female company, aside from relatives when he went back from time to time to Loudwater. These were Victorian times and life at Oxford had a rather monastic tradition. There were no female students, even if there was a large population of parasitic prostitutes. George's companions, his colleagues, and his teachers, indeed his whole world at Oxford was entirely male. (His first serious female relationship apparently began as he courted his first wife when he was 26.)

In any event, George's constant, almost exclusive focus in those years had to be his studies. Even with the relative personal freedom he enjoyed at Oxford, he never lost sight of his goal, which was to equip himself with the intellectual trappings to serve God and mankind, and probably more specifically, to be a teacher.

George was one of about 180 resident undergraduates in Christ Church, most of whom were taking classical courses. In his case he 'read' Greek and Latin classics, history, and political economy. Undergraduate teaching at Oxford (and Cambridge) was, and still is, centred on the tutorial, held to be the quintessence of an Oxbridge education. Tutors or dons, who were academics resident in the college, would see students individually to discuss their week's work, usually an essay, and their assigned reading. George probably had one or two tutorials a week, complemented by university-wide lectures and classes.

His three years at Oxford comprised nine terms, each lasting eight weeks, with vacations and study breaks in between. The total duration of the teaching terms amounted to less than half the year but he was expected to do academic work during the three holidays, known as the Christmas, Easter, and Long Vacations. Examinations were administered by university (not college) examiners and held in Oxford's huge and lavish new (opened in May 1882) "Examination Schools" building. Following the initial Responsions exam, George had to pass three more important tests. In July 1886, after his third term, it was classical "Moderations" or "Mods", which focussed on all the great ancient Greek and Latin authors. This was called the "first public examination". "Public" because other students could sit on the sides of the room and observe. That way the observers could get a better idea of what lay in store for them, but it also heightened the nervous anxiety of exam-writing.

After this, George became part of the "Honour School of Modern History" whose curriculum covered the history of England from the 5th century to modern times, as well as general European history and political economy, reading authors such as Aristotle, John Stuart Mill and Adam Smith. (A few years later, George would teach courses in political economy at Bishop's College in Canada.)

In August 1887 he went off for a two-month concentrated study break to the village of Silchester, located a safe distance from the tempting distractions of both Oxford and of his family in Loudwater. He needed to cram seriously for the next big test in October, called "the Greats", a series of lengthy and demanding written exams in his chosen areas of study. Finally, in June 1888, he sat for the "second public examination", "the Finals", which were three-hour written and oral exams taken over several days.

GPW, with his colleagues at Christ Church.

In the end, the results of all these tests and other challenges accumulated 3rd Class Honours for George. It must be acknowledged that this was not an outstanding score, and he may have been disappointed with himself. However it was academically quite respectable: The majority of students received only a 'Pass BA'. Christ Church had a reputation, not entirely deserved, for attracting casual, even idle students from wealthy or aristocratic families. Such a criticism could never have been applied to the serious and determined young George.

At the formal conclusion of his studies was a grand ceremony in Oxford's historic Sheldonian Theatre. On Saturday, July 7th 1888, as reported in *The Times* (in Latin, no less!) Oxford University conferred on "Georgius P. Woollcombe" the degree of "Bachelor in Arts" [sic].

What Oxford gave him

Beyond this degree, Woollcombe acquired at Oxford, and particularly at Christ Church, a whole set of attitudes, knowledge, intellectual paradigms, and a worldview that would be a central influence in defining his character and his future life. This related to areas as fundamental as religion, education, social divisions and social progress, and broad geopolitical assumptions.

Regarding religion, Woollcombe was of course very much a child of the Church of England. As a university student he was completely surrounded by Anglican influences. This was a far cry from the great variety of religions and philosophies that impact the lives of undergraduates today. At Christ Church, the office of Dean combined the headship of both the college and the Cathedral which was physically situated amidst the residences and The Hall. The great majority of students were Anglican; indeed up until 1855 only formally confessing Anglicans were admitted to Christ Church. Over the centuries many of the Church of England's bishops and theologians have been graduates of this college (including the renowned contemporary scholar, Rowan Williams, who was also recently Archbishop of Canterbury). Knowledge of religion, Anglican style, was interwoven into the curriculum. Moreover, resident students were expected to attend evening prayers in the Cathedral as well as the Holy Communion service on Sunday, which always included a sermon by one of the University's dominant theologians.

The influential voices Woollcombe would have heard and read were mainly conservative but increasingly, more progressive ideas were being expounded and listened to. For example, the liberal teaching of T.H. Green, a professor of moral philosophy who died just before Woollcombe arrived there, is widely recognized as the greatest single religious influence in Oxford in the second half of the 19th century. Green's legacy was to enhance the growing and widespread enthusiasm in England for implementing the social implications of Christianity, namely compassion and practical help for the needy. This trend must have influenced Woollcombe's belief system and strengthened his incipient idealism.

Of obvious importance to his subsequent career as an educationalist, Oxford shaped and sharpened his views on both the aim and the methods of a young person's education. The heavy emphasis on classical studies provided a complete view of ancient thought and civilization. This was seen by his tutors and professors as offering a stronger, more enlightened understanding of the modern world as opposed to a more technical, academically specialized approach.

It was notably pertinent to the teaching of history which was Woollcombe's primary area of study after passing his "classical Mods" in 1886. (In modern jargon, we might say he "majored" in history.) *The History of the University of Oxford* (Vol VII, eds Brock and Curthoys, 2000) notes that "Oxford historians [in the late 19th century] saw their curriculum as meant essentially to empower a generous conception of intelligent citizenship rather than to further a professional discipline." When it came to the objectives of education, one could say that Woollcombe emerged from Oxford more as a generalist than a specialist.

As regards educational method, the tutorial system of learning imbued in him the indispensable value of individual, direct teacher-pupil relations. This became a personal trademark of Woollcombe's style of teaching throughout his career. At the same time as tutorials, the crucial importance of major examinations had come to dominate the life of undergraduates at Oxford since the 1870s. This emphasis also stayed with Woollcombe in his administration of education at Ashbury.

The deep-rooted class divisions of English society, so evident at Christ Church and Oxford, must have impacted George Woollcombe's attitudes in this formative stage of his life. Almost everyone in England tended to be classified according to their family's social standing. The Woollcombe family was far removed from the high status of nobility or even aristocracy. Nor were they part of the new wealthy commercial class of those who were profiting from the industrial revolution and Britain's booming international trade. Traditionally, the Woollcombes were landed gentry from Devonshire. More pertinently, George's immediate family were in a respected social class of their own, the Anglican clergy. According to Oxford's admission records in those years, about a quarter of the undergraduates were sons of clergymen. Equivalent numbers came from families of landowning aristocrats, professionals (e.g. doctors, lawyers), and business owners and managers.

The influence of both the clergy and the aristocracy was even higher in Christ Church than in Oxford as a whole. So young George Woollcombe was comfortable and assured as he defined his place among his undergraduate colleagues and tutors. He knew who he was and who he wasn't, and he moved on from there. And while there surely was a traditional caste system prevailing in 19th century England, widespread social reform and democratization were moving ahead inexorably and changing the conservative social, religious, and political status quo. As it happened, Oxford scholars and graduates were in the intellectual forefront of both opposing camps – the progressive movement and the conservative resistance to it. Woollcombe was influenced and inspired by all this. His feelings must have been reinforced as he made his decision not to stay in the family mould, which was eminently conservative, but rather move to Canada.

George's worldview was given shape when Britain was at the height of its imperial standing. The Empire meant everything to any Englishman when he considered the outside world. For many Britons in the 19th century, the Empire was simply the evident manifestation of the inherent strength and virtue of the English nation. The British never questioned the superiority of their educational system of which Oxford was considered, at least by Oxonians, to be at the zenith. While the British may have had a less patronizing, less comprehensive approach to education in their colonies than the French with their *mission civilizatrice*, nonetheless a quasi-religious missionary zeal motivated many idealistic Oxford undergraduates who looked to social service and teaching in the colonies. These attitudes must have influenced young George Woollcombe as he considered his future.

As viewed by Canadians in the 21st century, however, Woollcombe's education had obvious cultural limitations, which he could hardly have appreciated. For example, the Oxford society of his time was culturally and linguistically homogeneous, quite the opposite of our universities today. But that was then and this is now. In the meantime, the whole world has been utterly changed by de-colonization, tectonic geo-political power shifts, massive migrations of people, and globalization. Students nowadays are encouraged to branch out interculturally and to learn new languages. While Woollcombe did bring some teaching of French and German into Ashbury, he was never comfortable speaking any language other than English.

These formative Oxford years were decisive in giving him a solid foundation of learning, in honing his personal values, and in shaping the intellectual and social attitudes that would inform his opinions for the rest of his life. In a real sense, George Woollcombe entered Oxford as a boy and left it as a man.

He was amply equipped with a first-rate Oxford education as he set out to begin his life's career.

III. Early Years in Canada

Crossing the Atlantic

After a summer of preparation, a fresh, confident and ambitious 21-year old George Penrose Woollcombe sailed off to take on the world. A lifetime later, in 1950, being interviewed by a journalist, he remarked that of all the many transatlantic voyages over his life, he best remembered his first. That one was from Liverpool to New York in the autumn of 1888. He claimed he paid only $40 but that treated him to a first-class passage. From there he took a train to Hamilton, Ontario where he stayed for a couple of months, presumably with some family friend. His career as a teacher began in January 1889 when he moved to the village of Lennoxville, Quebec. At the start of the winter school term, he took up a teaching position in a boys' English-speaking private school.

Why did he choose this path? His family background certainly did not suggest a military career, or government service, or commerce. He might have sought to be ordained and become a parish clergyman in England, as had his father, his two grandfathers and a great-grandfather. He would have had to wait a couple of years for that: in those days the Church required young men to have reached the age of 23 before being accepted as clergy. Or he might even have become a schoolmaster in England. Clearly he must have thought deeply about his mission in life as he set out on this adventure in the New World. Most fundamentally, he believed that God was giving him an opportunity to contribute substantially through being a teacher to the society that he was moving into. (In such a context George commonly used the word "Providence".)

Among other factors, he no doubt took into account his father's feelings. In all likelihood the Vicar encouraged George to go to Canada. Family members remembered the Vicar denouncing prevailing social and moral trends in England characterizing them as "Sodom and Gomorrah", while Canada in his imagination was "the Promised Land".

As far as we know, he had no specific knowledge of Canada; no close friends or family members had been there. Most likely, the Vicar saw Canada as a land of promise that was British but not England. His son would not be moving to a foreign country.

As well as the excitement of the adventure and his father's moralistic advice, the young man was likely driven by a still undefined altruistic goal that centred on educating the young. His ambitions were not aimed at material wealth. The remuneration of private schoolmasters in Canada would be a pittance compared to the salary an Oxford graduate could command in the British Civil Service or even teaching in good English schools, not to mention going into a commercial firm.

As it turned out, George had not abandoned the ecclesiastical vocation. He had just deferred it for a few years. He intended from the beginning to be ordained into the Church at some time in the future. In the meantime, he decided he would be a teacher abroad in the Empire. This was also in line with the influences and ethos of Christ Church and Oxford. With his decision to move to Canada, the seed of his future life's motivating purpose was planted. George was practical and determined, but he was also essentially an idealist.

The country he was entering was young. It was vibrant and expanding. Confederation was only twenty-one years old, the same age as George himself. Sir John A. Macdonald was nearing the end of his days; the Laurier era was soon to begin. George Woollcombe sensed, correctly, that his services would be highly valued in Canada. Canadians in the late 19th century, at least English-speaking Canadians, looked up to Britain and aped the English, particularly British education.

In all these ways, a world of hope, promise and commitment to high ideals awaited him. He may have sensed that this was his destiny.

Did he adopt Canada as his new country? The period in which Woollcombe left England for Canada was the apex of the grand Victorian era of British imperialism and of fixed, unchallenged social values and religious attitudes. Aside from the indigenous peoples and

Quebec's French-speaking population, the majority of those who came at that time to live in Canada, that is British North America, considered themselves to be British if not English. Throughout his life in Canada, Woollcombe remained English in his own mind. He talked of England as "home" and between 1888 and 1950 he made an extraordinary number of sea voyages, – eighty-nine to be exact, to and from England. This is a record likely few in Canadian history have matched.

And yet he put down his roots in Canada and became a significant member of Canadian society. He made his life's work here and here alone. He raised his family here and all his children were entirely Canadian, mind and spirit. As we will see, after retiring from Ashbury he tried to resettle in England, but it didn't work and so, now calling Ottawa "home", he returned to Canada for the rest of his life. In the end he died and was buried in Canada.

Beginning to teach

Woollcombe's move to Lennoxville was in response to an invitation from the Rector (headmaster) of Bishop's College School (BCS), the Rev. Dr. Thomas Adams, M.A., D.C.L. This was a British-style private boarding school, connected with the Anglican Church, in a remote rural, largely Anglophone enclave of Quebec, called the Eastern Townships, some 25 miles from the border of Vermont, USA. It had been founded half a century previously in pre-Confederation Lower Canada with the aim of serving the educational needs of "sons of English gentlemen", mainly wealthy Montrealers. The young Mr. Woollcombe would have felt comfortable moving into this cultural context, not least thanks to the man who hired him.

Adams was born in Australia and educated at Cambridge. He had assumed the joint responsibility of Principal of Bishop's College and Rector of BCS in 1885. The official BCS history records that "his humourous, unruffled, keen good sense got him a name throughout the Townships and beyond of being a man's man and one to bet on." The school grew in reputation and enrolment under his leadership. At that time, there were about 100 boys in the school, all boarders. Dr. Adams became Woollcombe's mentor and, in retrospect, a model for him as he launched his career.

Adams had engaged Woollcombe as the "Fourth Resident Master". His Honours B.A. from Oxford would have been seen by the Rector as more than adequate credentials for a junior teacher of schoolboys. For the young man starting out, the assignment must have been highly satisfying and no doubt he considered himself quite up to the challenge. We don't know but perhaps Adams had gone to England that summer to recruit teachers and had advertised his intentions among graduating young men at Oxford and Cambridge and elsewhere. (This was a practice Woollcombe himself would later adopt, when hiring teachers for Ashbury College.).

The school was physically located right beside Bishop's College (later Bishop's University) with which it was integrally associated. In Woollcombe's first few months in Lennoxville, Adams suggested to his novice protégé that he give a course of lectures in political economy to a few second-year students at Bishop's College, over and above his teaching at BCS. Successful in this assignment, Woollcombe was rewarded in June 1889 with a concurrent appointment as Lecturer in Political Economy. His salary for this was one hundred dollars a year. He had studied political economy at Oxford, and such academic knowledge was in precious short supply in Lennoxville.

Many years later when the history of BCS was written, an excerpt therefrom read: "Among the strengths of the Adams rectorship, 1885-1891, was the stability of a good teaching staff, ... masters of considerable ability". G. P. Woollcombe was one of six to be singled out in this regard. One of his strengths was his kind and individual attention to his pupils. He had quickly acquired a strong reputation and respect among the BCS staff and pupils and their parents. As we shall see, in the next couple of years this reputation would serve him well.

Young Woollcombe was clearly ambitious. Notwithstanding his promising start at BCS, he decided in 1890 to accept a new teaching job elsewhere. Again according to the official history of BCS, this move may have been prompted by the limited promotion prospects at the Lennoxville school.

The competing job offer came from the Rev. C.T.S. Bethune M.A., D.C.L., headmaster of Trinity College School. TCS was a similarly well-established private school and was affiliated with Trinity College, Toronto and the high Anglican Church. Its location was Port Hope, a small town on the north shore of Lake Ontario, essentially a railway stop on the road to Toronto. In September 1890, Woollcombe accepted the position of Assistant Master there. As before, he taught history (English history of course!) and Latin. The school life and curriculum in this boarding school was once again similar to 19th century English schools. However, as at Lennoxville, it had all the social and climatic challenges peculiar to rural, frontier Canada.

Again here, G.P. Woollcombe remained only a short time, just one academic year. He was soon called away to begin his life's central work.

1891 – "Mr. Woollcombe's School" is born

In the years following Confederation and its designation by Queen Victoria as the new country's capital, the small town of Ottawa was booming. Within a few years it had changed, as one contemporary writer put it, "...from a subarctic lumber village transformed by royal mandate into a political cockpit." Before government activity started to grow, Ottawa was already thriving as a centre for the lumber industry. It was scorned by Montrealers and Torontonians as backwoods, but it was a mainstay of Canada's economy. A start was being made to build infrastructure and social facilities to accommodate Ottawa's new economic and political status. One thing the new capital still lacked, however, was a good English-style private school for boys. Those who could afford it typically sent their boys away to boarding schools like BCS or TCS.

In the late 1880s this lacuna bothered several leading Ottawa citizens. Mostly they were so-called 'lumber barons' who were also closely connected with the Anglican or the Presbyterian Church as well as the ruling Conservative Party. Largely rough-hewn sons of poor English and Scottish immigrants plus a few Americans, they had made fortunes developing the local forest industry. As a whole they were not promoters of culture or even philanthropy, but they did want to empower their own sons with the right British education which they themselves never had. Many lived in mansions in Sandy Hill and had their offices near to each other along the south side of Wellington Street, facing the new Dominion's Parliament Buildings or on Sparks Street. This area was the very hub of Ottawa's power structure. They would discuss current concerns among themselves, often over lunch at the Rideau Club, also located on Wellington. The club members were Ottawa's elite. The Prime Minister, Sir John A. Macdonald himself was the club's first president.

So it was that early in 1891, while he was teaching at Port Hope, Woollcombe was approached by four or five Ottawa notables including the fathers of some boys he had taught the year before at BCS. They wanted to discuss the idea of starting a private school in Ottawa, and wondered if he would be interested. He had caught their attention with his qualifications and his teaching style, characterized by direct, personal attention to each individual student. They had considered his recognized success to date as a schoolteacher as well as his Oxford degree and his Church-of-England family background. He was only 23 at the time but his youth, far from disqualifying him, may have been seen as an advantage when combined with his obvious commitment and determination. Both headmasters, Adams of BCS and Bethune of TCS, gave him their strong personal recommendation.

Woollcombe was fascinated and excited by this prospect. He was more than happy to make plans to that end. Was his own embryonic vision for a lifetime of service in education already beginning to take shape? Was he now seeing before him the heady possibility of starting his own school? His own creation? In the following months he was introduced to several other prominent Ottawa business and church leaders who were prepared to support the project with their time, their influence, their money, and their commitment. In return, the new capital's elite would have a good school for their sons. These gentlemen would work closely with Woollcombe to set up the nascent school. The bright young Englishman would soon start to integrate into Ottawa life.

As winter turned to spring that year, great interest in the project by parents of potential students was aroused. Available student places were starting to be filled. By May 19th, Woollcombe was ready to place the following advertisement in *The Ottawa Journal*:

Private School for Boys

MR GEO. P. WOOLLCOMBE. B. A., graduate in honors of Christ Church. Oxford; assistant master at Trinity College School, Port Hope; and late assistant master at Bishop's College School, Lennoxville; intends next September to open in Ottawa a Private School for a *limited* number of gentlemen's sons

Boys will be received from the age of eight to fourteen, and will be instructed in English, Classics Mathematics and French. Ten boys have already been promised and an early application is desired. Apply to GEO. P. WOOLLCOMBE, B A. T C.S, Port Hope.

References kindly permitted to Rev. C.T. S Bethune, D. C. L, headmaster of T. C S., Port Hope; the Rev. T. Adams, D. C. L., rector of B. C. S., Lennoxville; the Hon. E. Dewdney, J. Gormully, Esq.

In the summer of 1891 Woollcombe moved to Ottawa, renting living quarters at 129 Maria Street (which later became Laurier Avenue West) near the corner of Elgin St. where the Lord Elgin Hotel is now. For the school classroom, he and his supporters rented a single room at the Victoria Chambers, perfectly located at 138 Wellington Street. on the southeastern corner of O'Connor, directly across the street from Parliament Hill. (A bronze plaque now marks this spot, put there on the school's centennial in 1991.)

Victoria Chambers. This was the birthplace of Ashbury College.

By September 1ˢᵗ the daily ad in *The Ottawa Journal* now read in part:

> *Mr. Geo P Woollcombe…receives a limited number of pupils…whom he*
> *prepares for larger schools and colleges. English, classics, mathematics and*
> *French thoroughly taught and an individual interest taken in each pupil…*

> *…apply Geo. P. Woollcombe, Victoria Chambers, or 129 Maria Street.*

On Wednesday, September 16ᵗʰ, 1891 at 9.30 a.m. the doors of the school opened. There were seventeen boys, aged between 9 and 15, in the one large upstairs classroom. A stern, dignified but kindly and approachable young man stood there at the door and welcomed each one by name. Most of them had not met him before, and were nervous. They had been told by their fathers that his name was "Mr. Woollcombe". Little did they appreciate what an historic moment this was. However deep down, G.P. Woollcombe himself probably did have such an inkling. This was the start of what became his life's project. His dream was materializing. His destiny was starting to unfold.

Since the school had so few pupils, albeit with a wide range of ages, Woollcombe initially chose to have only two classes, called 'forms'. Regardless of their age, he placed those boys who were somewhat advanced in their schooling into Form II and the beginners into Form I. For some subjects, such as spelling & dictation, history, geography and religious knowledge (called 'divinity') he taught both forms together. Other subjects he taught separately, such as mathematics, which comprised arithmetic, algebra and geometry (then called 'Euclid'), English composition & grammar, reading and Latin.

All the boys were sons and grandsons of businessmen (mainly in the lumber industry), parliamentarians, civil servants, and professionals. One of these boys was Charlie Tupper. He was the grandson and namesake of a Father of Confederation who was later prime minster, briefly in 1896. For several students, this was their first day of formal schooling, some having received instruction at home with their parents or a hired tutor.

Westward Macdonald. · Age. 13.   Form. I.

Arthur Rowley.   Age. '14.   · Form I

Percy Thompson   Age 12.   Form I

Davies. Dalton.   Age 13.   Form I

White. Hanley I   Age 15.   Form I

White Fred. II   Age: 13.   Form I

Charlie Tupper   Age 10.   Form II

Gormully. Robert   Age 11.   Form II (7

Watters, Rex.   Age 12   Form II

Anderson. Ernest Montague. · Age 10   Form I.

Anderson. Percy   age 9   Form I

Gilmour Kenneth   age 10.   Form I

Lambart. Fred: aged 10   Form I.

White: Louis   age 11   Form I

Ritchie I

Ritchie II

Palmer a. Z.

Camble

The first class list of 'Mr. Woollcombe's School',
September 1891, handwritten by GPW.

C. Tupper.

Private + School + for + Boys.

Ottawa, Michaelmas Term, 1891.

II. Form

	No. of Boys in Form.	Rank in Form.	Remarks	Master's Signature
DIVINITY.	16.	6.	Good.	Geo P. Woollcombe.
GREEK.				
LATIN.	9.	4.	works very well.	
LATIN COMPOSITION.				
EUCLID.	6.	3.	V. Fair.	
ALGEBRA.	6.	2.	Good.	"
ARITHMETIC.	5.	1.	V. Good.	
FRENCH.	11	1	V. Good	J. Fleury
GERMAN.				
READING.	7.	1.	V. Good.	J. F.
SPELL. & DICTATION.	16.	1.	Excellent.	
HISTORY.	16.	1.	"	"
GEOGRAPHY	16.	2.	Very good.	"
ENG. COMPOSITION.	9.	9.	a little weak.	"
WRITING.	—	—	Good.	
ENG. GRAMMAR.	9.	6.	V. Fair.	"
DRAWING.				
BOOK KEEPING.				

General Conduct V. Good.

Geo P. Woollcombe Principal

Next Term commences Jan: 6th 1892.

Charlie Tupper's first report card, January 6th, 1892.

Woollcombe soon engaged the part-time services of two other teachers who were well known locally. Monsieur Joseph-Marie Fleury, who had his *maîtrise* from the University of Paris, taught French. The Rev. Dr. Henry McKeekin taught writing and elocution. Woollcombe himself taught all other subjects.

"Mr. Woollcombe's School", as it was known, enjoyed a promising start. Its prospects looked good.

Wedding bells

By the time he had founded his school and established himself in Ottawa, George Woollcombe was ready for marriage – emotionally, professionally and financially. We have no record or indications relating to his social life in those years, outside of his life as a schoolmaster and principal-cum-entrepreneur. He was an eminently eligible bachelor, whether by Canadian or British social standards. What we do know is that on Sunday, August 1st, 1893 he married Julia Edith Dirom Acres in England.

A news item in *The Ottawa Journal* on August 26 got the story almost right:

> *"PROF. Woolcombe [sic], so well known in Ottawa educational circles, who went to England some time ago, has been married to an English lady and will not return here for several weeks longer."*

Although Julia's family background was quite different from that of George, she seemed ideally suited and well prepared to be his wife. For one thing, she and her family were already somewhat familiar with Canada. Her father, Charles Acres, then a British Cavalry officer, had been posted to pre-Confederation Kingston immediately following his marriage in 1860 to Julia's mother, Henrietta Coxworthy. Julia's maternal grandfather, Thomas Coxworthy, had also spent many years in Canada with the British Colonial Service, in Quebec City, Nova Scotia and Kingston, where he died in 1868.

Julia as a young woman. This photo was taken on a trip
to Ottawa, three years before her marriage to GPW.

Julia, just before her marriage.   Julia Acres, as a teenager.

Both the Acres' children were born in Kingston: John in 1861 and Julia in 1863. To provide historical perspective, Kingston had been the first capital of the newly merged United Province of Canada, from 1841 to 1844. In the 1860's was still an important military centre of the colony. It was also the home base of the rising star of Canadian politics, John A. Macdonald.

Soon after this assignment, the Acres family returned to England and settled in Plymouth, Devonshire, where Julia was brought up. We have little record of Julia's education or her life during her twenties. We do know that her father died in 1888, when she was 25, and she moved with her widowed mother to Liverpool. We also know that in July 1890 she visited Ottawa, where she had her photo portrait taken by a Sparks Street photographer. Perhaps she was travelling at the time with her mother who, we can imagine, might have wished to revisit that familiar territory.

We can only speculate on how and when George met Julia. Was it in some way through the Devonshire connection, common to both families? Were their parents directly involved in their meeting? That would not have been an uncommon practice in those times. And of course there was their common interest in Canada. Might the first meeting have occurred during Julia's trip to Canada in 1890?

George must have been smitten by her beauty. There are several photos of her in family files, one taken in Plymouth when she was in her late teens, the one previously mentioned that was taken in Ottawa at which time she was 27, and a third one probably taken at the time of her wedding when she was 30. Julia was indeed a strikingly beautiful woman. She had fine, strong, even features, high cheekbones, short dark hair, warm dark eyes and a thin but warm little smile. She was a mature woman, four years older than George, which probably attracted the serious, high-minded and ambitious young man. Both George and Julia were close to their mothers. Coincidentally and unusually, both mothers were named Henrietta.

Somehow in the midst of those busy creative years of founding his school, George found the time to court Julia and arrange for the wedding. There was much transatlantic correspondence and of course his annual summer trips "home" to England.

And what a wedding it was! The marriage was celebrated in Julia's and her mother's parish, All Saint's Church, Prince's Park, Liverpool. On the three previous Sundays, the vicar would have announced the impending union to the congregation, intoning in the liturgical language of the Church of England:

> "I publish the Banns of Marriage between Julia Edith Dirom Acres, spinster of major age, of this parish and George Penrose Woollcombe....This is the [first] [or second] [or third] time of asking. If anyone know just cause or impediment why these two should not be united in Holy Matrimony, ye are to declare it." And on the third time he would have concluded: "...or forever hold your peace."

Large family contingents of Acres, Coxworthys, Woollcombes, Jacobs, Colquhouns and numerous family friends were present for the joyous occasion. The service was conducted with appropriate dignity by the groom's father, the Reverend W. P. Woollcombe. An old newspaper clipping found in the family files gives a detailed account including all the wedding guests and how the principal ladies were dressed. Even the bountiful array of wedding gifts were listed (rather indiscreetly?) by the newspaper article: chinaware, silverware, crystal, fancy household items, plus a piano and several cheques, all designed to help set up a new home that would be appropriate for a respectable English lady and gentleman.

Worthy of note for our story was that among those present at the wedding was Miss Beatrice Colquhoun, who was Julia's bridesmaid. Nicknamed "Daisy", Beatrice was Julia's first cousin. Daisy's mother was the sister of the bride's mother. She also shared a similar colonial Canadian background, her father, Captain Isaac Colquhoun having also served in the Kingston area in the 1860s. This younger cousin and intimate friend of Julia was attracted to the groom's brother Fred

Woollcombe. It is said that many a romantic match has been ignited between guests at a wedding! Three years later she married him. The two newly-wed Woollcombe couples then became closely bonded, especially during the first few years the Fred Woollcombes also lived in the Ottawa area.

And so, generously equipped and lovingly sent off by their families and friends, George and Julia sailed from Liverpool soon after the wedding to begin their life as a couple together in Ottawa.

His brothers' keeper

Throughout his whole life, George Woollcombe's family held a central place in his personal priorities. At this point in his story, some details of his family life are in order.

After he moved to Canada, George remained in constant close touch with his parents, his sisters and his brothers. His family was tight-knit. He corresponded frequently with them and almost every summer through his life he visited them in England. He readily assumed active responsibility and caring concern for them, especially with his brothers. As the eldest, he felt this to be his unquestionable duty, all the more so since he was the first to become financially and professionally established in his adult life. The extent of his active involvement became evident over the next few years.

In due course, all four brothers followed him to Canada. The first to come were Willy and Fred. Some details and dates of their coming are unclear, but the approximate story is the following, pieced together from family lore and some precise historical records, such as the passenger lists of arriving vessels. Within a couple of years after George had moved to Canada and successfully started his career, the big question gripping the family was – what were Willy and then Fred to do? As mentioned, the Vicar believed he could not afford to send his other sons to university. Possibly he noticed a newspaper advertisement placed by an American entrepreneur seeking immigrant labour for his farms. In any event, the Vicar arranged for his two sons to go off to the USA. In 1890 they went as hired hands to work on a farm in a frontier town called Hillcrest, Iowa. At that time Willy was 21 years old and Fred barely 17. By modern standards this seems a somewhat heartless decision by their father. Perhaps his feelings about the prevalent immorality in England were a factor in his sending them off in this way. Apparently, also, he didn't mind that the United States was not British any longer.

The boys must have been excited by the adventure of it all. As it turned out, however, they did not enjoy their new life as farm hands, nor the prospects it offered them. In the spring of 1891, they fled northwards across the border to seek refuge and support from big brother George, who was teaching at the time in Port Hope. That summer they moved with George to Ottawa where he helped them both find employment. Two of GPW's strongest supporters and the fathers of students in the new school happened to be the top officers of the North West Mounted Police, Major Percy Sherwood who was the Commissioner and Fred White who was the Comptroller. Willy was delighted to join the force. He was soon assigned by the NWMP to Makinak, Manitoba. He remained in that province for several years, but as will be seen, his later moves raised eyebrows and caused considerable grief within the family.

For young Fred, George found a job as a clerk at the Union Bank in Ottawa. (This later became the Royal Bank.) The head office of that bank was just next door to the Victoria Chambers where the new school was located, and George knew the bank directors. Fred later moved to the bank's nearby Merrickville branch, and then to Norwood, near Peterborough. After that he moved with the bank to Goderich, Ontario where he raised his family of three girls.

Lionel was next in line to move to Canada, this time without a prior adventure in America. He came directly to Ottawa in 1895, aged 18. Again brother George found him employment, along with Fred as a teller in the Union Bank. Later Lionel married a Manitoba girl and moved with the bank to Rapid City, then to Minedosa, then Winnipeg, then with Eaton's in Toronto, and finally Lindsay, Ontario where he retired.

The last to come was John, the youngest brother, whom George hired some years later as a teacher at Ashbury following his graduation from Cambridge. John taught English and junior math for two years there. He then returned to England to pursue an ecclesiastical career. According to his son Philip, the pay for a schoolmaster in Canada at that time was too meagre for him. John eventually became one of his father's successors as Vicar of Loudwater.

Later on George involved both Willy and Lionel in his school, Ashbury College Limited, by way of selling (or perhaps giving) them shares in the company he formed in 1900.

A final word about Willy, who sadly became the black sheep of the family. Long years afterwards Uncle Willy was always spoken about in hushed tones around the family dinner table. Not long after moving to Manitoba he quit the NWMP and became a farmer for a few years at various small town addresses. Then at some point he moved back to Ontario and joined the army – the Royal Canadian Artillery. As the onset of the Great War loomed, he did not want to fight in Europe and he deserted from the army. In those days in Canada this was seen as a serious and odious crime. So Willy high-tailed it back out west where he moved around furtively. In 1916 in Winnipeg, he signed a legal attestation as "William Edward White". He gave his correct birthplace in Loudwater and correct birthday, October 5th, but gave the year of birth as 1872, four years later than the year he was actually born. He gave his next-of-kin as "Geo P Woollcombe, half-brother [sic] of Ashberry Cottage [sic] Ottawa". A copy of this attestation was found in the government archives.

Later Willy apparently settled in Prince Albert, Saskatchewan and changed his name again, this time to Woods. It was said he became a forest ranger, apparently for the rest of his life. Family contact was not entirely lost and over the years George and his wife would occasionally send parcels to "our unfortunate brother Willy", as George sadly called him. The last that was heard of him was after his death when a stranger appeared at the Woollcombes' door at Ashbury. She was a middle-aged Aboriginal woman and she claimed that for many years she had been "Willy's lady". She said that he had been a great success as a forest ranger and even claimed that a national park had been named after him. No reference can be found on the Internet to such a park, either national or provincial. Apparently she was not asking for money but just wanted to make the connection.

Ashbury House School

Since that September day in 1891 when his school's door opened, Woollcombe had made it clear that he harboured a higher ambition than a one-room day school. As he had told an Ottawa journalist at the time, he intended "as his classes enlarge to establish a permanent and much larger private boarding school." In the following years he struggled to nurture his newborn school. In 1892, eight more boys attended, and three more in 1893. For the 1893-94 school year with a total enrolment of 28, he rented two more rooms in the Victoria Chambers. These would not be nearly enough for the next year since he could easily plan on enrolment doubling. But he was faced with a dilemma: Where would he go? And how could he afford the adequate space he needed to expand?

The answer, at least for a few years, was soon found, and it was close at hand, just down the street. On May 2nd, 1894 a neighbour, Esther Sparks Slater died. Mrs. Slater was for many years the widowed matriarch of two historically prominent families, which gave their names to two of Ottawa's most central streets. Her home, at 186-188 Wellington Street, was a large four-storey house. It was spacious and of unequalled centrality in Ottawa. Mrs. Slater's daughter, Augusta Slater Currier, and son-in-law, James E.W. Currier lived next door at No. 190. The Curriers were also an important Ottawa family. They were already supporters of Mr. Woollcombe's School and they offered to rent their deceased mother's homestead to the school for the modest sum of $75 per month. They also decided to enroll their two sons Cyril and Dyson as students in the school. The boys' cousins, Leonard and James Slater, were already there. Until his death in 1985, just before he turned 101, Cyril remained a devoted and much celebrated Ashbury alumnus.

186 -188 Wellington Street.

This was the home of Ashbury House School, 1894 to 1900.

With this move Woollcombe realized it was time to give his school a name. He chose "Ashbury House School", after the Woollcombe family's ancestral manor house from centuries past. In this way he symbolically and permanently linked his two passions – his school and his family.

The Staff and Students of Ashbury House School in 1896

Top row, left to right — Ernest Montague Anderson, Harry McLean (killed in action overseas), Phillip B. Totler, Geoffrey G. Chrysler, Robert Devlin (dead), S. Robertson, Louis Malloch (dead), Cyril Currier, Delamere Magee and Allan Keefer.
Second row — Mr. Hickens (master), Thomas C. Keefer, Charles H. Tupper, Robert G. Gormully (dead), George Ferris, Leonard Slater (dead), Edward H. Stewart, Rex Walters, Arthur Smith, James Slater, A.Z. Palmer (dead), O.R. Dickie, Mr. Cyril McGee (master).
Third row — Louis T. White, J.A.C. Macpherson, Percy Anderson, Smith Henderson (dead), L.P. Sherwood, Louis Pattee (dead), Allan Dale Harris
Fourth row — Mons. M. Fleury (French master), Harry Wooding, J. Montague Bate, Horace Dickie (killed in action), Hugh N. Fraser, Walter Millen, Rev. G.P. Woollcombe (headmaster), J.A. Symes (dead), P.R. Moore (dead), E. Dyson Currier (killed in action), Elbert N. Soper (dead), Spencer Dale Harris (dead), Dr. McMeekin (teacher of elocution).
Fifth row — Philip H. Chrysler, A. Smith, Ray Avery, Charles Coursol (dead), Fred A. Blackburn, Alfred Warren Symes, Noel S. Fleming, Charles Malloch (dead), H. Nelson.

Ashbury House School. Students and staff in 1896.

In the new space, school enrolment did indeed bourgeon to 48 students in 1894. The school was to remain this size for the next six years. Another big advantage was the residence. Even before the actual move down the street, Woollcombe had started to advertise spaces for students in residence. Now he had the space and facilities to include ten such boys. From the beginning Woollcombe's dream was that his school would educate boarders as much, or even more than day-boys. This was the model he had grown up with and the dream he had nurtured since coming to Canada.

For the additional classes Woollcombe hired two more teachers: a Mr. Hickens and a Mr. Cyril McGee. He had enticed the latter to come to him from TCS, Port Hope, where they had been colleagues five years previously. Woollcombe himself kept an active daily teaching schedule, as he continued to do throughout his career as headmaster. Sports and physical education were a central priority in his approach to education.

The Ashbury boys would run around Parliament Hill across the street, and had their own small schoolyard with a hockey rink in winter on an empty Sparks Street lot behind the building. In 1895, a year after the school's move, Sparks became the first street in Ottawa to be paved.

These first years of Ashbury House School were as optimistic as the country itself: The mood was consonant with the times. The economy was surging again, and Wilfred Laurier had been swept into office in June of 1896 with his vision of the future for Canada. "The twentieth century belongs to Canada!" he famously proclaimed.

At home with Julia

In the meantime, with his marriage to Julia, George's own domestic situation changed significantly. By the spring of 1893, it was obvious to him that his bachelor's quarters in the rooming house downtown on Maria Street were quite unsuitable for a school principal with a new bride from England, especially if they would soon have children. He decided to look around in the residential district of Sandy Hill. Many well-to-do Ottawa businessmen, professionals, and government leaders had built grand Victorian-style mansions in this area, several of which still stand today as heritage buildings.

George found a fine home for rent, not a mansion which he certainly could not afford, but a row house, at 371 Daly Avenue. It was one unit of a handsome, three-storey stone structure, built twenty years previously and called Philemene Terrace. Just up the street lived Sir Sandford Fleming, the inventor of standard time and one of Ashbury's early benefactors. Possibly Fleming helped Woollcombe find the new home. Next door in the same building, at 369 Daly, lived Archibald Lampman, the famous poet. This friendly acquaintanceship with Lampman and his family was to endure. Lampman died in 1899, but a few years later his widow put their son Archibald Otto into Ashbury. Later, in 1915, Woollcombe hired the poet's brother-in-law, the Rev. Dr. Ernest Voorhis, as a teacher and school chaplain.

371 Daly Avenue, Philomene Terrace, where GPW lived with Julia in 1893 and 1894. Their first child, Philip, was born here.

On arrival in Ottawa in September of 1893 Julia and George moved right into their new home to begin their married life. They had planned a family and even before arriving in Canada, Julia was pregnant. In addition to coping with pregnancy, the autumn and winter were busy just settling in, making new friends and meeting her husband's colleagues and students at the Wellington Street school. On May 24, 1894 in their Daly Avenue home, she gave birth to their first child, a boy, Philip Herbert Penrose Woollcombe.

Thus, before his 27th birthday GPW had launched both his school and his family. These were productive years for him.

George and his little family were soon to shift their home again. Late in 1894, they took over the upstairs rooms of the big house at 188 Wellington that the school had moved to. Julia, with her new baby must have had mixed feelings about the move. The new quarters were dingy and ancient, compared with their relatively modern row house on Daly Avenue. However it was a much more convenient location, both for their family life and for running the school. George could be present there to attend to the many, incessant demands on his time, and Julia was now able to oversee boarding life. Moreover, no longer did George need to spend half an hour walking to work, or if he was in a hurry taking the tramway up Rideau Street – Ottawa's brand new electric railway! In any event, they were warm and comfortable in front of their fireplace on those cold Canadian winter nights.

That first winter on Wellington Street, Julia was pregnant again and on September 25, 1895 she bore their second child, a girl whom they called by the uncommon Welsh name of Maithol (Julia`s grand-parents were Welsh). Maithol's middle name was Henrietta, after her two grandmothers. George's recent bachelorhood now seemed a distant memory and his household rang with the sounds of babies.

Adding to the family atmosphere, George`s brother Lionel immi-grated that year. He came to Ottawa and for many months stayed with George and Julia.

During these years with Julia, George Woollcombe continued his annual practice of visiting England for three or four weeks during the of school holidays. He usually also took a holiday in the Canadian, or sometimes the northern U.S. countryside in the summer. With Julia he rented a cottage on the shore of Kingsmere, a pretty little lake, only a half mile long, in the Gatineau Hills close to Ottawa. This was the beloved summer playground of many Ottawa families, including several Ashbury supporters, such as the Bates, the J.R. Booths, the Slaters and the Gilmours. George and Julia would have found congenial company there. (A few years later, in 1902, a senior civil servant, then deputy minister of Labour, by the name of Mackenzie King became enamoured with Kingsmere, and purchased a large property nearby that became his summer residence for the rest of his life.)

**GPW and Julia with their son Philip, 1½ years old, and
daughter Maithol, 3 months old. Christmas 1895.**

Available records show George and Julia took up summer residence
in Kingsmere in 1895. The previous year, what with the birth of Philip
and the move of the school and their residence to 186 Wellington, they
had no time to indulge in a summer cottage. On June 20, the little family
set out from Ottawa's Union Station on the recently opened railway line
to the little station at Chelsea, Quebec. There they hired a carriage to
take them along the dirt road through Old Chelsea to their cottage. On

September 7, they returned to Ottawa by the same itinerary in reverse. In the meantime, George felt he had to go off on his own to England for the month of July, leaving Julia, Philip, and a maid to fend for themselves at Kingsmere.

While Julia managed this quite well, she insisted with her husband that the next summer would have to be different. She too wanted to go back to her mother country. On August 1, 1896, the whole family, now with two children, set sail for England. During their absence, George left his brother Lionel in charge at Ashbury to handle any significant correspondence or queries from students' parents or potential parents. The proud mother and father wanted to show off two-year old Philip and baby Maithol for the first time to all four grandparents, plus numerous uncles, aunts and cousins. Moreover, of course they were there for the wedding of George's brother Fred to Julia`s cousin Daisy. Fred and his bride soon followed George and his family back to Ottawa where they set up house a few blocks away on Maria Street.

The next summer, 1897, they were back at their Kingsmere cottage. Again Julia became pregnant. But, alas, that would be the last of their pleasant summers together.

Tragedy!

Those were good and exciting years for George Woollcombe. By the time he turned 30, he had made his name as a successful school principal. His school was growing and already valued for the quality of education it offered. It had a strong base of support from the Ottawa community, including many leading figures of the country. And he had a happy and healthy new little family at home. However, before the century was out, a full store of tragedy would descend upon him.

Expecting their third child, in the autumn of 1897 George and Julia asked both their mothers to come from England to stay with them in the winter of 1898. Fred and Daisy, who were also expecting a baby, their first, did so as well. As noted, Julia's and Daisy's mothers were sisters. The three expectant grandmothers came to Ottawa for several months, and the extended family reunion was full of joyful anticipation. Fred and Daisy's daughter Gladys was born on October 29 and all went well. On New Year's Day 1898, the three Woollcombe brothers sent a card with their portrait, taken by a local Sparks Street photographer, to their absent father in England. This photo was in George's personal files when he died in 1951.

These are the two sides of a New Year's greeting card that the Woollcombe brothers, (L to R) Fred, Lionel and George sent to their father.

Julia's third pregnancy was difficult, but initially the birthing was successful. On the 1st of April a lovely, healthy baby girl, Phyllis, was born. (She was destined to play a central role in the last decades of GPW's life). Tragically, Julia suffered serious complications following childbirth. On May 9, Julia died, leaving her children and husband and mother with their terrible bereavement. This extraordinarily beautiful woman whom George had loved with growing passion suddenly was gone.

His mother Henrietta stayed to console George and to help out as long as she could. However, her husband, in retirement in Kent, was also in fragile health and she had to return to him, leaving George to manage by himself. Within a few months, on March 26, 1899 William Penrose Woollcombe, the old patriarch himself passed away. The mantle of family leadership now fell on the young widower's shoulders. George could not get back to England to help his mother cope with the situation until that summer. Henrietta herself had not much longer to live. Tragedy soon struck again. On June 7, 1900, George received a telegram that his beloved mother had just died also. His triple bereavement shook him to the core.

Henrietta consoles her son and grandchildren
following the death of Julia

A poem he subsequently penned and signed shows a side of George Woollcombe few in his life ever saw. In uncharacteristically shaking handwriting, the words reflect the acute despondency that had seized him. One might expect to find these morose feelings more in an old man approaching death than in a young man moving up in the world. Still, in face of his tragic circumstances it does reveal him to be intellectually disciplined and in full control of his mind, however shaken he was emotionally. He kept this poem in his personal papers and shared it later in life only with his and Julia's son Philip. The title he gave the poem and the last stanzas suggest he may have written it some time later.

"Looking Backward"

— § —

I look across the bridge of time
O'er spanning many a weary year.
And down my cheek there steals a tear
*   I know not why.*

— § —

I see myself a merry child
With heart and soul untouched by pain.
Oh! Would those years might come again,
*   And last for aye.*

— § —

I see the budding joys of youth
(How eagerly I clutched at them!)
But they were tender, frail, and slim,
*   And withered soon.*

— § —

Love met me. To its sweet embrace
My trusting heart I gladly gave.
And joy passed o'er me like a wave
*   Engulfing all.*

— § —

E'en as a wave it passed away
And left me callous, cruel, cold,
I've grown defiant, reckless, bold
*   To all mankind.*

— § —

The time has passed long long ago,
Since I expected joy to find.
Life to my weary jaded mind
*   Is nothing worth.*

— § —

Soon, soon, I trust will come that peace,
Which yet remains for even me
For death's pale phantom form I see
*   Not distant far.*

— § —

Geo.P.Woollcombe

It was an expression of George's strength of character that his inner turmoil in this difficult period of his personal life was kept strictly private. Never had he known such searing grief, and he never would again, to the end of his days. Yet, as we shall see, his work as school principal and entrepreneur continued with more energy and initiative than ever.

IV. The Argyle Years – Evolution and Growth

The new century

As the 19th century came to an end, George Woollcombe might have paused briefly to look back over the 33 years of his life so far. Despite family tragedy, he may well have felt some early gratification with the course he had set and with his achievement to date: the fulfillment of his driving motivation to become an educator in his new country; the successful launch of his lifetime project, a high quality boys' school on the English public school model; his own new and growing family; and above all, as he saw it, his service to God through service to society. These confirmed the directions he had established at the outset. His rudder was firmly fixed.

The turn of the century was also a turning point in Woollcombe's life story. The century's first decade was to witness major departures in his life story: his second marriage and two more children, the relocation and bourgeoning of his school, the start of his career as an ordained minister of the Church, and significant new academic achievements.

By 1900, the challenges facing this young man were enormous. He had critical decisions to make regarding the future of Ashbury House. Overseeing and guiding fundamental changes in the size and nature of his school required vision, determination, and constant attention to detail.

Weighing on George even sooner and more acutely than his school were the sudden and tremendous new responsibilities for his three very young and motherless children. Soon after Julia's death in May 1898, he urgently needed to make new household arrangements. The MacPherson family who were sympathetic friends and Ashbury parents had helped out by taking care of the toddlers, Philip and Maithol, but only for a while. Sister-in-law Daisy and brother Fred were there to help, but they had their own infant, and George needed permanent female support at home. Also a full-time nurse had to be hired for baby Phyllis.

Widower GPW's children (L to R) Maithol(5), Phyllis(2), Philip(6), early 1900.

Jessie to the rescue

Without realizing it, George had already met the one person who, together with his deep faith, would be his chief pillar of support and strength for the rest of his life.

Jessie Mickle was a teacher of English and Mathematics at Miss Harmon's School for Girls, which was something of a sister school to Ashbury House. It was located a few blocks southeast on Maclaren Street at the corner of Elgin Street. She had moved from Toronto to Ottawa and started teaching there in the autumn of 1897. In the normal course of her professional life in this small Ottawa community, she met George Woollcombe. They soon established a friendly relation-ship. During those last two years of the century, as George coped with his dreadful personal grief and household challenges, Jessie gradually and very gently became a close, supportive confidant and, as much as discretion and her own work allowed, a practical help for him with his children.

Jessie Mickle, school-teacher.

She came to be part of his life outside of Ashbury. She may even have visited his apartment over the Wellington Street school. She likely met George's brother Fred and Fred's wife Daisy, who lived nearby. In August 1899, when Philip was only five, George took his son with him to England, and the boy remained there to stay with a family friend. When this arrangement did not work out, Jessie was able to arrange for one of her older sisters to bring Philip back home to Ottawa.

Unlike the Woollcombes, Jessie's family had long been established in Canada. Her grandfather was Charles Julius Mickle, of Scottish stock but living in England near Oxford. In 1832 he moved with his family to Upper Canada. For only three dollars an acre he bought 640 acres of land in Eromosa County near Guelph, cleared land for a farm and built a family homestead. His oldest son, also called Charles, who was 20 when they moved to Canada, quickly established his own pioneering leadership by building up a lumber business based in Guelph and then later in Gravenhurst. When he was 32, the younger Charles married another second generation Canadian, Ellen Thurtell, who was only 17. Over the next 24 years Ellen proceeded to bear him thirteen children, all of whom were born in the old Mickle homestead. Jessie was born June 16, 1865 and she was Number 12. Families were large in those days; we recall that George's mother Henrietta had twelve children.

All the children of Ellen and Charles but one, who died in infancy, were highly educated and successful in their respective professions: Two were noted physicians, two married physicians, one was a lawyer, one was a mining engineer, one married the Dean of Science at the University of Toronto, one was a noted painter and Associate of the

Royal College of Art, one took over and expanded his father's lumber business, one was General Secretary of the Women's Foreign Missionary Society of the Presbyterian Church, another was president of the Women's Canadian Historical Society. As noted above, Jessie was a teacher. In 1879 after Charles Mickle died, Ellen moved the family home from Guelph to downtown Toronto. Jessie, who was then 14, continued her schooling there and attended Normal School in Toronto.

Jessie as a young woman.

She was the perfect match for this struggling, lonely, young widower and father who was also an ambitious and rising school principal. She was mature, modest, well educated, sensitive, capable, and a devout Christian. In George's perspective, Jessie had been sent to him by Providence.

And so, on Wednesday July 11, 1900, George Penrose Woollcombe wed Jessie Marion Mickle in the Anglican Church of the Redeemer at Bloor and Avenue Road in Toronto. The church's minister, the Rev. F. E. Howitt officiated at a very simple ceremony befitting George's recent state of mourning. For example, unlike for his first marriage seven years earlier, publishing the Banns of Marriage was dispensed with. The wedding was attended, however, by several of Jessie's family, her formal witness being her dear niece and friend Ethel May Ellis. George's witness ("best man" in modern terms) was his brother Lionel. George was 33, and Jessie was 35. Following these quiet nuptials, the newlyweds took the train back to Ottawa to begin their happy and productive half-century partnership.

His persona evolves

There was a significant evolution in the persona of G.P. Woollcombe in the years following the death of Julia and with his marriage to Jessie. His appearance changed to a more solemn demeanour when he shaved off his moustache, which he had worn since teen-age years. His premature balding had progressed rapidly. Soon he would be wearing a clerical collar and be known as "the Reverend Mr. Woollcombe". A decade later, he would have no hair at all on his scholarly pate. Photos taken over these years show an increasingly stern, resolute and intellectual figure, albeit still youthful. This outward bearing reflected his growing inner maturity as he overcame his personal, tragic losses and moved on in life. He was determined to pursue his dominant ambition, his school, while sealing his union and raising a family with his life's partner, Jessie.

GPW in 1900.

His maturing seemed also to be accompanied by a more complete acceptance of Canada as his country. The "Canadianization" of GPW was evident by the time his British wife Julia died. On that very day, May 9, 1898, he purchased a plot of 100 square feet in Ottawa's Beechwood Cemetery. Julia was the first of all his subsequent family, including himself, to be buried there. A significant influence in this regard was his new wife. While Julia happened to have been born in Canada by an accident of history, her upbringing, education and family background were entirely English. Jessie, on the other hand, was third-generation Canadian with deep roots and attachments here. She had never lived outside of Canada.

Yet this should not be construed as a transformative shift in his own sense of identity: Canada was definitely and permanently his home, the location of his work and his life, but in his view he had not moved to a foreign country. Canada remained for him largely an extension of Britain, however fully he became integrated in and adapted to the Canadian social and economic life of his time. When he travelled in the summers to England, he talked of "going home". But he also talked of "coming back home" to Ottawa.

A busy summer

George Woollcombe's vision, commitment and determination were evident in his planning and handling of the school's relocation in 1900. Ashbury House School was flourishing in every way but there was a problem. The Wellington Street location could not handle more than 47 or 48 pupils. With Ottawa's rapidly expanding population (now 65,000) there was a pressing demand for more admissions. Moreover, that old house had proved barely adequate for boarders, and certainly not for more than ten. Consequently, despite the current tumult in his family life, Woollcombe was again planning a major move. After discussing the matter with his closest supporters, he started looking for a new location. In the course of 1899, he thought he had found one, a twenty-minute walk from Wellington Street, south along Metcalfe Street to Argyle Avenue. There he found a large, yellow-brick, three-storey house on a 15,000 square foot lot at 70 Argyle Avenue. It seemed to be what he needed, so he started negotiating its purchase from the owners, Annie and Edward Skead. Finally, on May 3, 1900, after arranging a mortgage loan, he paid them the huge sum of $9750. This was soon paid back to him by his financial supporters but in the meantime Woollcombe had received title to Ashbury's new home.

70 Argyle Avenue. Site of Ashbury College, 1900 to 1910.

This was just the start of what was to be a busy, momentous summer. First he had to wrap up the school year in its old location. Thirteen boys graduated that year. In the few weeks following his 33rd birthday (May 21st), he mourned his mother's death (June 7th) attended to her estate and comforted his brothers in Canada and sisters in England. With his lawyer, John F. Orde, he arranged for the incorporation of the newly named Ashbury College on June 14. He organized its first shareholders' and board of directors' meetings, held on July 4. He prepared for his wedding to Jessie Mickle in Toronto, married her on July 11 and brought her home to Ottawa. Next, he relocated his whole school as well as his family to the splendid but inadequately furnished big house a mile away. He then oversaw in detail not only the refurnishing and equipping of the Argyle Avenue house but also the radical transformation of his school's legal and institutional character.

That summer, exceptionally, he did forego his annual trip to England!

The Ashbury College Company Limited

Now that GPW had become a substantial property owner and was set to expand Ashbury's operations considerably, he was advised to convert his hitherto small family business into a legal corporation and to set up a proper corporate structure. It was also appropriate, Woollcombe believed, to revise the school's name to reflect this development. He chose the formal name of the Ashbury College Company Limited. A board of directors was duly elected, and Woollcombe became the secretary-treasurer and managing director. He held this position for many years and remained on the Ashbury board until his death 51 years later.

Of course he was not alone in the leadership of this venture. The first subscribers and board members comprised a veritable 'Who's Who' of Ottawa notables. But two men stand out as pillars of support: William Horsley Rowley and John Fosbery Orde. They were by far Woollcombe's closest business associates and confidants in Ashbury's earliest years.

W. H. Rowley was a senior and influential businessman. Born and educated in Nova Scotia and a graduate of the Royal Military School in Halifax, he had moved to Ottawa in 1875 as a rising young employee of the Merchant's Bank of Canada. However, like most of Woollcombe's supporters, he made his fortune in the lumber industry. In 1887, he joined E.B. Eddy, a Hull, Quebec pulp-and-paper company. He soon became the firm's first secretary-treasurer. On the death of Ezra B. Eddy in 1906, Rowley became president and guided the company's fortunes until he himself died in 1915.

Over these years, Rowley had become an active leader in various business associations, such as president of the newly formed Canadian Manufacturers' Association. Politically, he defined himself simply as a strong supporter of all projects he believed would advance the interests of Canada and Canadians. In Macdonald's time he was a Conservative; with the turn of the century and change in governmental colours, he supported Laurier and the Liberals. In the Anglican Church he was a lay delegate to various church synods and treasurer of Christ Church Cathedral. His residence in the two decades before he died was the magnificent stone mansion, Stadacona Hall, on Theodore Street, now Laurier Avenue East. This previously had been home to Sir John A. Macdonald before the Prime Minister moved to Earnscliffe. (At present, Stadacona Hall's unlikely owner is the High Commission of Brunei.) Conveniently for Rowley, it was almost next door to Laurier's house.

Not least of Rowley's activities was his patronage and financial leadership of the newborn Ashbury College. From the very beginning he had been one of the prominent Ottawa citizens who encouraged the young George Woollcombe to start a school for boys. After helping Woollcombe move Ashbury to Argyle Avenue, he became chairman of the newly incorporated company's board of directors and the largest subscriber of capital. Rowley's son Arthur was one of Woollcombe's original seventeen pupils in 1891 and a few years later his sons John and Roger also attended the school. In 1894 Woollcombe asked Rowley to be godfather of his son, Philip. He was indeed Woollcombe's strongest supporter and above all a faithful friend.

John F. Orde was Ashbury's lawyer from the beginning and for long years thereafter. Born a Maritimer, his family moved west when he was a boy. He took his secondary schooling at the Ottawa Collegiate Institute, studied law, and in 1891 was called to the Bar of Ontario at the tender age of 21. He was soon recognized and accepted as a rising legal star. Although three years younger than GPW, by the time of Ashbury's move to Argyle and legal incorporation in 1900, the soundness and expertise of his legal advice were crucial. Like Rowley he nurtured his connections with the Anglican Diocese, with the lumber industry and with the Conservative Party. Orde became director and legal counsel of the new corporation's board. Like most of the board members, he was also an Ashbury parent.

As well as 'Secretary-Treasurer and Managing Director', Woollcombe was of course 'Principal'. Note that for several years this title was used interchangeably with 'Headmaster'. For the next twenty years it was primarily Rowley and Orde who responded to Woollcombe's initiatives. Together this triumvirate essentially ran the business side of GPW's school. The board meetings were held in the principal's office at the school on Argyle, and after the move to Rockcliffe, in Orde's office on Sparks Street. In 1906 they were joined by wealthy Ottawa industrialist James W. Woods who became Vice-Chairman. Woods' company initially manufactured lumbermen's supplies and it grew into a business empire across Canada. His son John had entered the school in 1903.

Settling into Argyle

In the course of the remaining weeks of summer 1900, the Woollcombe family moved into their new home, and Jessie and George began their life as a married couple. All the inherent strains and radical adjustments were compensated by the excitement, the challenges and the shared vision of the new life before them. As they set out on this adventure, they had no time for doubts. After seeing to the essential needs of their children and themselves in their new quarters, they had to prepare the school, including the residence, for the opening of classes in early September. Jessie was just as much involved in this huge task as George.

Ashbury attendance was growing, which indeed was the main reason Woollcombe had decided to make the move at all. From 47 boys at Wellington Street the previous term, there would now be 58, including 13 boarders. Eighteen of these were new students. Administrative arrangements had to made, including payment of fees ($72 per year for day-boys and $316 for boarders). After all, Ashbury now was legally a for-profit corporation and, while making profit was hardly his objective, Woollcombe needed to keep the school financially afloat.

The old house was poorly equipped for the school's purposes. It had been the private home of the Skead family. Woollcombe needed to move quickly to acquire and set up adequate furniture for the classrooms, dormitories, kitchen and dining room. At the first board meeting in July he had obtained authority to spend up to $820 for this purpose but the total cost for further improvements to the building in the end amounted to well over $2000. Then a new furnace was required, and a small gymnasium was added. Two years later he had an entire additional wing built on the back of the house, to the tune of $3000. All these expenses were approved by the board without question.

Ashbury College staff and students, 1902.

Kitchen and household staff had to be hired, which Jessie largely handled. Two faithful teachers who had been with George from the beginning remained after the move: French teacher Monsieur Joseph-Marie Fleury and elocution teacher Dr. Henry McKeekin. However, for the large school, more teachers were needed. A Mr. Lewis, newly graduated from Oxford, became resident master joining the Woollcombes in the school building, Herr Boettger from Leipzig would teach German and Mr. Emery drill and gymnastics. Woollcombe taught everything else in that first year in Argyle, as well as setting or approving the curriculum for the other teachers.

A big improvement over the Wellington Street location was the availability of more space for playing games and physical training. Aside from a yard behind the house there was an the expanse of field directly in front of the school, across Argyle Avenue. Soon, in 1905, this field was purchased by the government to start building the Victoria Memorial Museum. Now it is the Canadian Museum of Nature. It was to be Ottawa's first museum and was designed to complement in its Gothic style the Parliament Buildings at the opposite end of Metcalfe Street. Ashbury boys and staff would watch with interest while 300 skilled stonemasons brought here from Scotland constructed the massive structure. Ashbury continued to use the surrounding space for some years as a playing field.

Family life in Argyle

The Woollcombes were fully integrated into school life in Argyle. They had their meals with students and staff, although there was an alcove in the school dining room for the headmaster's family table. Their apartment was on the upper storey. The family became somewhat less omnipresent when in autumn 1905, they moved a few doors down the street to a rented house at 88 Argyle. The headmaster kept his office on the ground floor of the school building where he worked at his desk and received staff, students, and official visitors. Here also was where Ashbury's executive board members would meet. He received outside visitors at regular hours.

A notice in the Ottawa Citizen dated December 3, 1903 read:

ASHBURY COLLEGE, ARGYLE AVENUE OTTAWA
A school for Day and Resident Boys
The Headmaster will be at home from 12 noon to 3 p.m. and from 7 p.m.
daily except Saturday
N.B. Preparatory class for very young boys

The Woollcombe children too were part of the school life. On moving into Argyle in September 1900, Philip, the eldest at six years old, started his schooling and entered Form I. Later the two girls, Maithol and Phyllis, also were included in classes. This little known fact is interesting since Ashbury did not become co-educational for another eighty years! Moreover, it did not take Jessie more than a few months to add to the Woollcombe family. She gave birth to Edward Mickle Woollcombe on November 24, 1901. Their last child, George Andrew Woollcombe, was born while they were still living in the school building, on June 13, 1905.

George and Jessie valued their broader family connections even though all their relatives were far from Ottawa. They stayed in close touch with George's brothers, Lionel and Fred and their families, who had moved away, and with several of Jessie's siblings who were mainly in Toronto. They even tried not to lose all contact with George's wayward brother Willy who had disappeared out West. George arranged to bring his youngest brother to Canada: In September 1904 he hired John V. Woollcombe, a fresh Cambridge graduate, 23 years old and unmarried, to teach English and junior math. John was given quarters in the Argyle house. He stayed only two years before returning to England to marry, to become ordained and finally to end up as Vicar of Loudwater, just like his father.

Naturally the Woollcombes' social life during these Argyle years was mainly related to the school life. Church-related activities were becoming increasingly important, but most of George's personal friends were supporters of the school, and often parents of his students. He was admitted to the Rideau Club in 1908, where Ottawa's business and political elite would meet socially; the cost of membership was justified as a part of his constant and continuing need to nurture support for Ashbury, especially financial support and enrolment.

His philosophy of education

In his Headmaster's Report to the school Closing in June 1907, G. P. Woollcombe articulated and clarified his philosophy of education and his policies. It tells us a lot about him and his vision for his school.

At the outset he set out his basic objective:

> *...as the years pass we like to think that Ashbury is becoming not merely an old established and permanent institution of our city life but also is more and more, with increasing efficiency and thoroughness doing that work in our midst that evidences itself not merely in increasing numbers, not merely in the intellectual successes of its pupils but chiefly in the successful development of such a character in those who sit within its classrooms as shall cause them to grow up to be men who with heart and soul fear God and honour their King.*

Then, following this statement of high ideals, George Woollcombe's pragmatic, business-like side, which looked to school enrolment, came to the fore:

> *And yet, granting that an institution is humbly and quietly striving to do this work, increasing numbers necessarily means increase in influence, and I am glad to state that... our numbers this year have been greater than in any previous year since the School's foundation...and we anticipate that our attendance roll next September will be considerably longer.*

He then made a number of other statements of his policies:

Reflecting his constant, active, personal concern for each individual boy's progress while a student at Ashbury, the headmaster observed:

> *While we are glad to welcome older boys to our class-rooms ... it is much more satisfactory to have the training of a boy from the beginning of his school days, and to pass him upwards through the school from the lowest to the highest Form*

Hard work, discipline, respect for authority, 'manliness', these were unchallenged core values at Woollcombe's school:

> *...there has been manifest throughout all the classes a spirit of work that accounts for so much in real progress and advance.*

> *...the influence of the elder boys has been on the side of true manliness and right. And as I have remarked on other occasions, when the elder boys are actuated with the true spirit of loyalty to authority, we inevitably find that spirit prevalent throughout the School.*

The importance of parents:

> *...there is a very serious responsibility attached to the parents of day-pupils. Where a boy lives at home, however earnest and devoted in their efforts his Masters may be, their work will be largely nullified if it cannot be supplemented by home influence.*

Thoroughness, regularity, effort:

> *It is not the boy, however naturally clever, who from time to time makes spasmodic spurts who eventually succeeds, but the boy (even though he be of moderate abilities) who from day to day, from week to week and from year to year works regularly with the least possible interruptions to his studies...*

> *...a boy to succeed must be in earnest, must be thorough, must be regular in his work...and possess a capacity for taking pains. And these qualifications form the true essence of a real school education.*

For Woollcombe, academic and athletic excellence was a matter of doing one's best: this was fundamental:

> *While we congratulate those boys who obtain the coveted honours, yet the winning of a prize is not by any means the sole test of a boy's intellectual*

advance...Progress is oftentimes marked by results that cannot always be set down on paper, but which is, notwithstanding, one that is very evident to those who day by day are watching a boy's intellectual and moral development. If there has been an improvement in method, in steadiness of work, in personal interest in study, while the outward results may not, as yet, be markedly visible, it is these characteristics that in the long run will tell in a boy's career

Sports and physical education:

...the physical training of boys is, and should be, complementary to the training of the mind. 'Mens sana in corpore sano' holds with special force in this age of restless activity and of mental stress.

The boy who is good at sport will usually be high up in his classes, while the boy who loafs on the playing field will too often exhibit the same attitude in the classroom.

...the attitude that we constantly strive to instil into the boys with regard to their sports is that which makes the one supremely important thing about a game, to be a straightforward manly effort, and not the mere victory in a contest by fair means or foul.

I think sometimes parents do not sufficiently realize the value of this branch of our work, nor of what great importance it is the bodily development of their children.

His view of Canada:

There is, I fancy, no country on earth which has better or greater opportunities for young men to rise to success and to make names for themselves than has this, our fair Dominion.

Finally, the Headmaster expressed his most heartfelt advice to those boys who were graduating:

May you carry with you into your new life, and what is more important, seek to put into practice, those principles that we have striven to instil into your character here. Strive to be good citizens, not only of the British Empire, but also, and chiefly of the Kingdom of Heaven.

Some of Woollcombe's expressions, concepts and values sound out-of-date, archaic to modern ears: 'fear of God', 'honour the King', 'manliness', 'loyalty to authority', 'the British Empire', 'our fair Dominion'. Moreover, accepted approaches to education have obviously evolved greatly over the past hundred years. Woollcombe's approach reflected his own Victorian-era formative years as well as the conventional social aspirations and attitudes of his time. His leadership and his direction of the school were viewed with respect and admiration by all his contemporaries.

Nonetheless, shining through the century of change, the central values of Woollcombe's approach remained valid. Speaking to the school many years later at Ashbury's 50th Anniversary in 1941, he reflected on his 42 years as Head. As he had done in June of 1907, he addressed his last words to the graduating class:

May I suggest to you two words to carry with you as you enter into this larger life. First the word 'efficiency' can describe 'doing one's best' and to do one's best inevitably means struggle, effort and self-sacrifice. But if you really do your best physically, mentally and spiritually, you find yourself becoming more and more efficient, more ready to cope with difficulties that may present themselves and more prepared for the work, whatever it may be that is set before you.

And the second word to carry away with you: 'service for others'. Let your efficiency be directed towards the helping of others. There will be two ideals that will always be set before you: the one, egotistic, to do the best I can for myself, for my own interest, my own welfare. To look after number one. And the other ideal, altruistic, to do our best to help others. To follow the first ideal may and probably will put more money in your pocket and will increase your social standing. But it will not assure you genuine success or real happiness. On the other hand, if you follow the other ideal and devote your lives to the service of others, you will discover real satisfaction and true happiness, and you will be following in the steps of Him – our Supreme Example – who once said "I am among you as He that serves".

In this way G. P. Woollcombe summed up the guiding values of his own life. His life's work was his endeavour to instil these values in his students: His message in short was: do your best, and serve others.

Becoming Reverend

It was during the Argyle years that George Woollcombe formalized his role as a man of the church. Of course he was born and bred in the Church of England. Before him, his father, both his grandfathers, even his paternal great-grandfather had been ordained Anglican clerics. His family home where he grew up was a country vicarage. His significant teachers and mentors through his education and early professional life as an educator were Anglican clergymen. And when in 1902 he sought permission to be ordained, his degree from Christ Church, Oxford was judged to have met the Church's formal requirement that postulants be graduates of an accredited theological college. The presiding bishop who interviewed him found that Woollcombe adequately met the standard stipulated at that time in church rules, the canon: that the candidate should be "learned in Holy Scripture, and sufficiently instructed in the Latin tongue".

Before becoming a "priest", one had to be ordained as a "deacon" by the bishop, and Woollcombe achieved this step on December 21, 1902, at a regular Sunday morning service at St. George's Church. Since the Wellington Street days St. George's, located close by on the corner of Metcalfe and Gloucester Streets, had been the Woollcombe family parish. The Church of England in Canada was a dominant religious denomination in those days, at least among Anglophones, and St. George's had become the largest Anglican parish in Ottawa. Woollcombe had established a respectful relationship with the long-serving rector, Rev. J. M. Snowdon, and Snowdon had asked him for help. As soon as George became a deacon, Snowdon appointed him curate, that is to say, an assistant to the rector.

The (newly) Reverend G. P. Woollcombe, 1903.

After the requisite one-year wait, George was ready to be ordained priest. Again it was the venerable and revered Bishop of Ottawa, Charles Hamilton who performed the laying on of hands at St. George's Church. It was Sunday morning just before Christmas, December 20, 1903. George was no doubt accompanied by Jessie and likely their four children. They made their way up snowy Metcalfe Street for the big event, probably by hired sleigh taxi.

According to a report in *The Ottawa Citizen*, "The service was of a very solemn character and impressed all who attended with the sacredness of the work of the minsters of the Gospel...There was a large congregation." The bishop preached the sermon, and the men's and women's choir sang "a sweet and truthful rendering of the anthem 'O, for a Closer Walk with God.'" Rev. Bogert, as archdeacon of the diocese, formally presented Woollcombe to the bishop. Several other clergy also assisted, including the bishop's son, Rev. Harold Hamilton and, of course, the rector, Rev. Snowdon.

This marked another step towards fulfilling George Woollcombe's life ambition. His persona and his own sense of self-identity were updated: From that time on he was referred to as "Reverend" and he always wore his clerical collar. For the rest of his long life he continued as an active clergyman in Anglican parishes.

He remained with Snowdon at St. George's until 1908 when he moved as curate to All Saints' Church, on the corner of Chapel and Laurier in Sandy Hill. In January 1913, when the chapel of the newly built Ashbury building in Rockcliffe was ready, he left All Saints' and integrated his sacerdotal duties into his school leadership at Ashbury.

It should be made clear at this point that while Woollcombe was solemnly ordained "priest" on this occasion, he almost never would have used this title, but rather "minister" or "clergyman". "Priest" was much too Catholic. In those days, the prevalent, mainstream view among Anglicans was a very distinct and sharp differentiation from Roman Catholics, in both doctrine and form. In the minds of all concerned, this was a very important division of Ottawa society, indeed of Canadian society generally. Anglicans saw themselves unquestionably as "Protestants" (however much their creed asserted their belief in "One Catholic and Apostolic Church".) They considered themselves much more akin to the Presbyterians, for example. Marriage to a Catholic was often shunned, and for some it could be a matter of family shame. Public education in Ontario was divided into the Catholic and the Protestant systems, entrenched in the Canadian constitution, the British North America Act. For most Anglicans in England and Canada and even more so for Episcopalians in the U.S., these generalized feelings of antipathy to the Roman Catholics and "all their papist ways" were intensified by their reaction against the Oxford Movement, which grew up in the mid 19th century and favoured much closer ties with the Catholic Church.

In George Woollcombe's case, his own family was definitely opposed to the Oxford Movement. His father, William Penrose Woollcombe had been appointed Vicar of Loudwater in part because he was explicitly "not a very high churchman". George was not "low church", but considered himself mainstream Anglican - "congregational" or "evangelical". The St. George's congregation had suffered a bitter schism one decade previously. Some thirty parishioners of high church persuasion parted ways and founded a new parish a few blocks away. George's in-laws, the Mickles, were strong Presbyterians. After joining the Church of England when she married George, Jessie always specified that she was "congregational".

The Lennoxville connection

Ever since October 1888 when young George Woollcombe stepped off the boat in New York City, and soon set out for Lennoxville to start his career, he had nurtured a special relationship with Bishop's College and Bishop's College School. He taught courses at both the school and the college. Even the invitation to start a school in Ottawa in 1891 was spurred on by the recommendations of his mentor, the Bishop's principal, Dr. Thomas Adams, as well as by the Ottawa-based parents of some of his BCS students.

In the first years of the century he renewed this connection. In the academic year 1904-1905 he taught a course as a lecturer in political economy at Bishop's College, thus drawing on his Oxford academic training. Despite the burden of his work in Ottawa he still found time regularly to make the four-hour train journey to Lennoxville to teach his classes.

The next year, on June 21, 1906 he was awarded a Master of Arts degree by Bishop's. Woollcombe's M.A. was essentially an honorary degree, directly related to his 1888 B.A. from Oxford. He did not study to get his Master's degree. He is recorded in the Bishop's records as a lecturer but never listed as a student, and his name does not appear on the register of examination results. Oxford's traditional practice was then and has always been to award an M.A. to Oxonian B.A. graduates after a minimum seven-year delay, and without further study or examination requirements. This practice was extended by Oxford to include certain other universities as the formal granting body. In this way, Bishop's enjoyed an arrangement with Oxford whereby it could so honour its own faculty if they happened to have an Oxford B.A. The term used for this practice between universities is *ad eundem*. (In Latin, *ad eundem gradum* means "at the same degree").

From that day on, Woollcombe made sure he would be known as "Rev. G. P. Woollcombe, M.A." He even quickly revised the letterhead on Ashbury stationery to reflect his new status.

In short, Woollcombe had had both significant experience as well as professional rewards in Lennoxville over the years since 1888, and he still had many friends and admirers there. This background helps us understand how a crisis in the life story of G. P. Woollcombe, and of Ashbury, suddenly erupted onto the scene in 1909.

Grave temptation

Nearly two decades after leaving Bishop's, Woollcombe was in his prime as headmaster of Ashbury. His school was becoming a significant Ottawa success story and it was virtually a one-man show. Moreover, it was on the cusp of a major expansion and relocation to Rockcliffe, for which Woollcombe's leadership was indispensable. However, early that year the Lennoxville school's headmaster had resigned. The BCS board believed their old friend and colleague to be the most suitable possible replacement. They urged Woollcombe to accept their invitation. On April 29 he dropped a dramatic bombshell on the Ashbury board. He announced that he had decided to accept the BCS offer. The decision seemed irreversible. To the Ashbury directors' chagrin, it was even reported that very evening in *The Ottawa Journal*:

> *Rev. Geo. P. Woollcombe, a graduate of Christ Church College, Oxford, who has occupied the principalship of Ashbury College in this city, since he founded the institution eighteen years ago, at a meeting of the corporation of Bishop's College, Lennoxville, was elected headmaster to succeed Dr. Bidwell.*

The dramatic consequences were instantly obvious to all at Ashbury and the board's distress was existential. The Rockcliffe project, already in an advanced stage, had to be aborted. All the related plans were changed or dropped. The board would need to begin right away with the impossible task of seeking Woollcombe's replacement. The Ashbury world was suddenly turned upside-down. The bubble of optimism and enthusiasm was shattered.

Within two months, however, to the huge relief of all concerned, Woollcombe changed his mind. At the next board meeting on June 24, he made a firm commitment to stay on. He was even able to announce an unexpected profit of over $5000 on the past year's school operations, and he personally subscribed to 147 more common shares in the corporation. Mercifully, the crisis was averted and the move to Rockcliffe was back on track.

What had been going through G. P. Woollcombe's mind over these months? Did he really want to abandon completely his major life's work at this promising stage and launch out on a new course? His decision to leave Ashbury was hugely disappointing to his many supporters and friends who had invested so much of their time, energy and money. It seemed so abruptly contrary to the values he had preached and up to now practiced: loyalty, steadfastness, commitment. How to explain it? Woollcombe must have agonized and wrestled with the matter over weeks, moving back and forth between the pros and the cons. He must have borne in mind several considerations. Unfortunately, he did not keep a diary, or if he did, it has not survived him. Nor is any relevant correspondence available.

Probably long-term financial security for him and his growing family was a factor. He was not well paid by Ashbury, especially considering his heavy leadership responsibilities. In 1905 he had agreed to a contract with the board (actually signed only by Rowley and Orde) which set his salary at $1200 annually for that year, rising to a still meagre $1500 by 1907 and onwards. This compared at the time to $1800 for a high-school principal in Ottawa, rising to $2600. He did have free quarters and board for his family and himself and free tuition for his children but there was no retirement pension provision. From his upbringing in England and throughout his life in Canada, Woollcombe had been used to very modest financial means. His school catered on the whole to better-off families, but he fully accepted and never complained about his own financial status. We do not know what salary terms he was offered by Bishop's, but since that school was supported by established Montreal wealth it is likely they were more generous. Ashbury's future, while bold and exciting, must have seemed less secure financially than that of Bishop's.

It is also probable that Woollcombe was attracted by the prestige of this long-established institution in Lennoxville. Ashbury on the other hand was just getting started. Ottawa in those days was still considered something of a backwater, compared to Montreal and even to Montreal's hinterland, which included Lennoxville.

Perhaps Woollcombe also tried to justify his decision, at least to himself, by noting that he had already spent many years as Ashbury's head, eighteen in fact. That length of time when spent in one institution seemed to be a respectably lengthy portion of any professional educator's career. Naively, he may have felt that moving on after such a period would not raise too many eyebrows.

While always motivated by high-minded ideals, Woollcombe had shown himself in his life decisions to be highly ambitious. He may have inwardly thought: "Here I am, nearly 43 years old, with recognized and substantial achievements already behind me. But now that I have the prospect of more security for my family and prestige for myself, why should I not make the jump?" All these considerations combined with the flattering approaches no doubt made to him by the BCS board may have heightened the temptation to the point of being irresistible.

(One of Woollcombe's successors at Ashbury, Ogden Glass, the school's fourth headmaster was faced with the almost identical entice-ment in 1950. But Glass succumbed. He left Ashbury to be head of BCS and later principal of Bishop's College.)

What were the countervailing factors in George Woollcombe's mind that ultimately won the day? The short-term impact on his family must have been in the forefront. His son Philip was nearly 15 and would be entering his final year at Ashbury, not the best time to suddenly change schools. Perhaps Woollcombe considered leaving him in boarding at Ashbury but the next school year was foreseen as transitional and some-what disruptive with the impending move to Rockcliffe. New arrange-ments would have to be made for the girls – Maithol, 13 and Phyllis, 11. Edward who was 8 would be in his third year of school, so perhaps not a major problem. And young Georgie, only 4, should be all right, mainly in the hands of his mother. But on the wisdom of the move to Bishop's from the family's point of view, the feelings and independent opinions of Jessie would be decisive.

Perhaps Woollcombe did not fully grasp the extent to which the move to Rockcliffe could not proceed without him. This project was no longer a "gleam in his eye" but was already well advanced and was driven by his leadership. His principal financial supporters, particularly James Woods and J.B. Fraser, were committed to the plan and had made large investments in it. They surely put great pressure on their man not to "abandon his ship in this moment of distress" as they might have put it.

Indeed, the central consideration holding Woollcombe back from going to Bishop's must have been the planned move to Rockcliffe.

The staff at Ashbury, the parents, and even the students could not have hidden their dismay at the news in April, or their joy and relief in June. We can never know, but likely the most powerful influence on George Woollcombe in that spring of 1909 was Jessie. He would have shared with her all his concerns and feelings, and his mulling over of what to do. She was always of a nature to bring out the practical considerations of situations. She might well have advised him to be true to his basic values: steadfastness and commitment to a high cause. She would have said, "Let's stay here at Ashbury."

V. Rockcliffe

The big move

The idea of moving to a larger more suitable location was a seed that had been planted and nurtured in GPW's mind from the very beginning. Woollcombe had told a journalist soon after his school opened back in September 1891 of his firm intention, as his classes enlarged, "to establish a permanent and much larger private boarding school." He wanted to serve humanity in this specific way and was driven by this ambition. The two previous moves, first to 188 Wellington Street and then to Argyle Avenue were stepping stones along this way. By 1906 his personal life had successfully settled into cruising gear. Happily remarried, he now had five children, an established status in the Church clergy, distinguished academic achievement, and a school, his own creation, that was flourishing.

Argyle was adequate for a few years of Ashbury's early development, but the school was outgrowing the constraints of an old, downtown house. From an enrolment of 48 on Wellington Street, Argyle was able to take in 53 in 1900. This had increased rapidly to 70 by 1906. It went on to grow to 80 in 1907, and finally to 97 in 1909. GPW's dominant concern at that point was not only overall enrolment but the limitations on the residential capacity of the Argyle building. Central in his long-held vision was that Ashbury should essentially be a boarding school. From his perspective, education of boys was more complete and more effective when the students were present in the school full-time. Argyle did house a few more boarders than Wellington, fourteen in 1900, and the numbers increased slightly, to sixteen in 1906. When in that year Woollcombe moved with his family to a rented home down the street, there was room for a few more so by 1909 twenty-two boarders were squeezed in. However, more than three quarters of the school population were day-boys and GPW's residential school ambitions were being frustrated.

In addition to the boarding constraints at Argyle, a broader concern was physical space for the whole school to grow outside as well as inside the building. Woollcombe envisioned extensive sports fields, and open grounds for other outdoor activities surrounding a large well-designed building with adequate classrooms, a dining room and kitchen, a gymnasium, and of course a chapel, as well as larger and more appropriate residences for students and staff.

So the first question was where should Ashbury move to? As GPW considered a future location, Rockcliffe quickly became the obvious choice. In the first decade of the 20th century, the Laurier years, Canada was booming and Ottawa was growing quickly. Centretown had filled up, as had Sandy Hill which had become the primary residential area for businessmen, politicians, and civil servants. On the other hand, Rideau Hall, the social epicentre of the Capital's elite and governing class, was surrounded by vast expanses – hundreds of acres of largely vacant fields. They had been the lands of Thomas McKay, the wealthy pioneering businessman and founder of Ottawa. McKay had built Rideau Hall as a home for himself and his family before it became the Governor-General's residence in 1865.

The Rockcliffe area was just starting to see some comfortable homes being constructed although mostly it was forest and pasture land. By 1910 there were only some sixty houses in all of what is now the Village of Rockcliffe Park. Roads were being built, although few of them paved, and Ottawa's new electric street-railway had run lines up Sussex Drive past Rideau Hall right up to where present-day Lisgar and Buena Vista Roads meet. For Woollcombe, Rockcliffe also had the advantage of being still distinctly rural. For many practical, aesthetic and economic reasons, he concluded this area might become an excellent home space for the Ashbury community.

In the course of 1906 and 1907, GPW increasingly shared these thoughts and intentions with his closest supporters and friends. All agreed to the emerging plan. The students and staff started to get excited. By October 1907, senior master Reginald Smith who was

editor of the school magazine, was encouraged by GPW to editorialize
as follows:

> We hear rumours of the intentions of the authorities to move the School to
> a place in the country, and indeed this change cannot take place too soon. It
> is unnatural that the abundant energy of our youthful members should be
> confined to such a small playing field....

Woollcombe's next big step was to find and acquire an appropriate
site. One fine day, soon after his annual trip to England in August 1907,
he set off by streetcar to look for a new location for his school. The sale
of the McKay Estate lands was in the hands of a syndicate called the
"Rockliffe [sic] Property Company". He quickly came upon a large lot
that satisfied his hopes. It was essentially an open cow-field, not culti-
vated and with a few trees and forested areas around it.

Essential to the process, of course, was the concurrence of his inner
circle of supporters: J.B. Fraser, Lt. Col. D.T Irwin, and James Woods
as well as lawyer Orde, who also played a central role. While ensuring
these individuals were kept constantly informed and in agreement, he
proceeded to initiate a round of negotiations with the syndicate's real
estate broker. By November 13, 1907, he was offered "...the Westerly
10 acres of block 10 of the McKay Estate for the sum of $12,000. The
sum of $3000 cash and the balance in three equal yearly payments at 6%
per annum."

Through dint of intensive canvassing, at which task he excelled,
Woollcombe raised the requisite subscriptions from twelve of Ashbury's
strongest supporters with deep pockets, in exchange for preferential
company shares in the school. Woods had had some doubts about the
proposed deal, but soon came around. On December 30, with Orde
beside him, GPW signed the "Agreement for Sale."

As soon as Ashbury had acquired the land, Woollcombe turned to
his next big challenge: – constructing on it a building appropriate to
his grand vision for the school. Through the year 1908 he discussed
various ideas for a desirable structure and in December he selected the

Ottawa firm "Weeks and Keefer". Allan Keefer was a rising Ottawa architect who had attended Ashbury House School on Wellington Street and who already had a good reputation for style and competence. From Keefer's plans GPW commissioned a large comfortable building in classical "Elizabethan" style, with mainly red brick exterior. It was designed for well over one hundred students, predominantly boarders, and ample facilities for academic, athletic and extra-curricular activities. In late June 1909, after Woollcombe had reversed his dramatic, not to say catastrophic, decision to resign, the Montreal construction company of "Byers and Anglin" was contracted to build the school, supervised by Keefer.

In the meantime, much more revenue was needed. While the directors of the company (Ashbury's board) collectively were responsible, their policy decisions were always at the initiative of GPW. The onus for fund-raising as well as for building the school was squarely on Woollcombe himself, with legal and administrative services provided by Orde. The cost estimate just for the building, although initially $50,000, was negotiated down to $44,000. When all the extras, including a gymnasium, as well as landscaping, plumbing and sewage, furniture, architect's fees, and so on were added in, over and above the $12,000 for the land, the total project would cost $87,567.

Woollcombe solicited funds in various ways, the most significant being subscriptions to debentures with 5% annual interest. Through 1909 and 1910 he systematically nurtured his contacts with members of Ottawa's moneyed class, most of whom had sons at the school or some other personal connection. He got the job done.

So it was that G. P. Woollcombe undertook and completed the most challenging project of his life: the purchase of a totally undeveloped 10-acre lot in rural Rockcliffe, the construction there of a large modern school building, the relocation of his entire school and the establishment of a new way of life for Ashbury College. It all happened very rapidly, and throughout the whole process, GPW was at the controls.

In retrospect, the two-month agonizing crisis in the spring of 1909, GPW's sudden resignation, was only a hiccup in this major story.

Work on construction started that summer of 1909 and proceeded apace for the next fifteen months. The cornerstone was laid in September and the new building had a roof by November, before snow fell. In June 1910, as soon as the school term at Argyle was over and that old house was put on the market, Woollcombe moved boarders as well as his own family over to Rockcliffe into the new building. The interior work was still going on as they moved in. Then, on the morning of Tuesday, September 14, with enormous excitement for everyone, the first term in Rockcliffe began.

The splendid new building in Rockcliffe, 1913.

One essential component of Woollcombe's ambitious and visionary project remained incomplete: There was no chapel. Chapel was always seen by him as the spiritual core of school life. However, by early 1912, the requisite additional fundraising, again entirely handled by GPW, was realized, and construction had begun again. More classrooms below and beside the chapel were also included. On January 19th, 1913 the chapel was officially opened for religious services.

G.P. Woollcombe could happily survey his spectacular modern new building and grounds surrounded by forest and cow pasture. He could rightly take satisfaction in knowing that an auspicious new era in his school had well begun.

Social networks

A good part of George Woollcombe's success in advancing Ashbury College – and specifically in fund-raising – related to his skill in networking. As founder and principal of a school with an outstanding and growing reputation in Ottawa, one where many of the city's top businessmen and professionals chose to send their sons, he was widely known and highly respected. His serious, determined demeanour and his clerical collar also helped. He capitalized on his reputation by developing and nurturing direct, personal contacts, even friendships, with a wide number of actual and potential donors and parents. His pleas for financial assistance were always courteous but also passionate and sustained. He was well known for quietly but consistently putting the touch on any well-heeled friend of the school. For this reason, with good-humoured resignation, some said they wished they could avoid running into him. These on-going connections served not only to bring in revenue, but equally to attract new students and maintain those already enrolled.

What sort of persons made up this community of Ashbury supporters and friends? In good part, the lumber industry dominated the Ottawa's business world. A strong majority of the shareholders of Ashbury College Company Ltd., both in numbers and financial weight, were lumber barons. Consider these names: J.B. Fraser, W.H.A. Fraser, J.W. Woods, W.C. Hughson, J.R. Booth, W.H. Rowley, Albert Maclaren, John Gilmour, W. C. Edwards. Beyond these lumbermen, other important supporters were lawyer J.F. Orde, Lt. Col. D.T. Irwin, coal merchant F.A. Heney, Sir Sandford Fleming, J. Roberts Allen, wholesale grocery magnate Sir Henry N. Bate and his sons, and a number of others. All of these prosperous individuals GPW could call on whenever his school needed them. Moreover, they all sent their sons and grandsons to Ashbury.

The social context for this networking was Woollcombe's increasing role within the city's elite. One notable event in this regard was his invitation to join the Rideau Club in 1908. The Rideau Club was founded in 1865 by Sir John A. Macdonald, the club's first president, and Sir George Etienne Cartier. Membership was always both sought-after and expensive. Over the years, and certainly in the first decade of the 20th century, it was the preferred and exclusive meeting place of Ottawa's political and business leaders. This is where most if not all the aforementioned Ashbury patrons had the habit of getting together for lunch and discussing their individual and collective concerns. It was therefore natural that the Reverend G. P. Woollcombe, M.A., Principal of Ashbury College, however modest his personal income compared to most other members, not only wanted to join the club, but was warmly welcomed into the sanctuary,

Woollcombe also nurtured his connection with Rideau Hall. The previous section described the Governor-General's residence as "the social epicentre of the Capital's elite and governing class". GPW's relationship with the vice-regal residence, particularly after the move to Rockcliffe, will be discussed in a subsequent section. We may simply observe here that Rideau Hall became another locus of his networking on behalf of his school.

In telling his story, we must take care not to compartmentalize the various parts of Woollcombe's life. In reality they were in the nature of a harmonious whole. His church life exemplified this. When he was ordained deacon in 1902 and then priest in 1903, his parish was St. George's Anglican Church in Centretown where he was the curate for six years. This church was an easy distance from both the school's locations on Wellington Street and then Argyle Avenue. He and his family and his Ashbury boarders could walk to attend Sunday morning services.

However, by 1908, as the move to Rockcliffe became imminent, he became increasingly attracted to the idea of changing to a new parish. The construction of All Saint's Church in Sandy Hill on the corner of Laurier Avenue (then called Theodore Street) and Chapel Street had been initiated and entirely paid for by Sir Henry Newell Bate in 1900. The Bate family were significant Ashbury supporters and several Bate boys attended the school. A number of other prominent families of the Ashbury community were All Saint's parishioners, including GPW's old friends W.H. Rowley and J.F. Orde as well as James W. Woods, whose mansion home was right beside the church on Chapel. The hard working first rector, the Rev. A.W. Mackay (rhymes with tacky) was a strong imperialist, a prominent Mason and a believer in practical education. He was only too happy to invite Woollcombe, who was just his kind of man, to assist him as curate. And GPW, the natural networker, was delighted to make the move.

Life and work in Rockcliffe

As we have seen, Ashbury's move to Rockcliffe and the establishment there of a brand new campus marked a turning point in the narrative of G.P. Woollcombe's life. Living and working in Rockcliffe, year after year for more than two decades until his retirement in 1933, this is where he consolidated his life's achievement. Taking this period as a whole, let us look at his way of life there: his home; his daily routine; Jessie who was his chief pillar of support; his relationships with the students, with the teachers and other staff and servants, with the Board directors, parents and Ashbury supporters. We'll deal with various events and issues that impacted his life and his leadership over this time. If ever there was an omnipresent, fully engaged school principal, it was G. P. Woollcombe.

The new building was designed, at Woollcombe's request, to have the headmaster's family home become an integral part of the school. It was the western wing of the school building, called the 'Annex'. It is still fully intact, now used for school administration offices. With their five children, aged from five to sixteen when they moved in, George and Jessie were quite comfortable with their new physical arrangements. There was ample space for all on the three storeys, and the Woollcombes thought it appropriate to invite one junior school teacher, Miss Edie Edwards, and a few very young boarders to live in rooms on their third floor. The heating, lighting and plumbing (except for initial water supply problems) as well as fire-safety were up to the most modern standards of the day throughout the building. Such a contrast to Argyle Avenue! Their home, as their daily life, was interconnected with the school by a short corridor on two storeys.

The Woollcombes lived in the Annex for their first seven years in Rockcliffe. In 1917, in order to give room for more boarders, the family moved a block away along Mariposa to a house at 2 Cloverdale Avenue, rented for them by the school. In autumn 1923, they went into to new Headmaster's House, just constructed on the school grounds.

A day in the life of the headmaster

On a typical school day, George Woollcombe would awaken at 6.30 a.m. or earlier with a tea tray brought by Jessie. After dressing he would go directly across to his study-office, located just inside the front entrance hall and to the left as one enters. Connected to his office was the smaller office used by Miss Emma Hamell, his secretary, who was also the school bursar. (He was loud in his praise of Miss Hamell, calling her his "financial fortress".) In the early morning he worked there alone, while the rest of the school was getting started. He would personally deal with his correspondence, writing often a whole stack of letters by hand. Only by about 1920 did he resort to using a typewriter. This confirmed his philosophy that a personal approach was preferable, although Miss Hamell would type some of the letters for his signature before dispatching them.

At 8 o'clock sharp he crossed the corridor to the dining room to have breakfast with the boys and the resident masters. According to one contemporary account, if anyone slept in and was late, nothing was said to him, but "G.P.'s eyes nailed him at the door and stuck with him until he sat down." Colloquially, but respectfully, everyone referred to the headmaster as "G.P.", or simply "the Head." At 9 o'clock, the whole school went to the Assembly Hall (which is now called Rhodes Hall) for roll call.

Many years later G.P.'s son George, who had started at the school in 1911, recalled,

> *"What stood out in my mind was the complete control my father had over the boys, as illustrated by, we'd all be in assembly there, little boys and middle boys and older boys, and he would never come in until they were all in assembly. Then as soon as he came in everybody kept quiet, just like that. He was a slight, relatively short man, about 5'7", but his presence, even at large gatherings would always be noticed and would inevitably result in an almost immediate reduction in the general hubbub."*

After roll call the boys went upstairs to the chapel for Prayers, led by Rev. Woollcombe, from 9.05 to 9.15. Classes were then held until 3.30 p.m., with a one-hour break for lunch (called "Dinner"). The Head was in a classroom teaching for one or two hours every day. This way he could ensure that he maintained contact with all his students. The rest of the time he could be working in his office, or consulting with students, staff, parents, or others. He was solicitous and encouraging toward the smaller boys and never failed to stop and speak to any of the students as he wandered the corridors.

He loved to walk. At mid-day sometimes he would stride for a good forty minutes to get downtown for lunch on school business at the Rideau Club and take the streetcar back. Later in the afternoon, after classes, there were sports (football, hockey, cricket), cadets and other extracurriculars, all of which G.P. followed and sometimes monitored closely. Often he would be in his study, reading, consulting with masters, seeing individual boys, counselling them and administering the prescribed discipline. After the day-boys went home, there would be supper (called "Tea") followed by evening prayers in the chapel and evening study (called "Prep").

Woollcombe usually had the evening meal in his home, spending time with Jessie and the children. But he would frequently come back to the school to "go the rounds" as he called it, visiting various boarders' rooms before lights out and checking on the work they had done. Many years later an old boy nostalgically recalled that reassuring voice: "Well, goodnight my boy, and now lights out." It remained for the housemaster on duty to see that the lights had indeed been turned out. The Head would then come home, usually read a bit, chat with Jessie and retire to their bedroom. Occasionally he would work late into the night in his office on correspondence or students' reports. Finally, every night before sleeping he would kneel down beside his bed to say his prayers.

Jessie, his closest partner

In many ways Jessie was just as involved day by day in school life as her husband, as well as raising their five children. For a full twenty years it was her role to manage, oversee and often directly undertake the whole housekeeping function of this residential school. She had charge of practically all domestic affairs. She had a strong, if quiet personality; it was she who set the rules and the tone.

The day she hired Fred Oliver illustrates this nicely. Over more than forty years Oliver was Ashbury's faithful and irreplaceable jack-of-all-trades. He started in 1911 when the school was just settling into the new Rockcliffe campus. He later recalled how Mrs. Woollcombe had employed him:

> *"...I kept my appointment to see Mrs. Woollcombe the next day. I found her a very kindly lady, very frank in the matter of business for she left me feeling there was work enough for three men to be done and was honest enough to*

leave me no other impression on the matter. She said the work was hard, the hours long, and the wage small but could be increased sometime in the future. I had answered her many questions to her satisfaction and listened patiently to the list of duties for the morning part of the day..."

Jessie Mickle Woollcombe, GPW's closest partner.

Jessie closely supervised the whole school kitchen operation: everything from ordering and preparing the food, ensuring sanitary conditions (for example, she would see that the butcher did not throw a horse blanket over the meat he was delivering by cart or sleigh!), having the filtered well-water analysed regularly, checking on the supply of milk from Bossy the cow (which grazed on the school grounds for a couple of years), ensuring the proper peeling of potatoes, hiring a new kitchen maid, to handling the cooking at the boys' winter bonfires near the toboggan slide.

On top of her children's active home life, Jessie involved them whenever she could in the Ashbury life beyond their classes and sports. (The latter were more the direct concern of their father.) Philip was in his final year at Ashbury after they moved to Rockcliffe. The two teen-aged girls, Maithol and Phyllis, attended Ottawa Ladies College. Edward entered Ashbury in 1907 and young George in 1911. Each stayed in school for nine or ten years.

Here is another story from Oliver's memoir, revealing of Jessie's hands-on style:

> "Madam, a very busy lady herself, like the Head, had no excuse for idleness. There was a time for play, and a time for work... After school had closed for the summer term and vegetables and fruits came into season, Mrs. Woollcombe got the young folk of the family gathering firewood for pickling and preserving. By the time school was ready to open there would be dozens of sealers or pickles and jams, marmalades and jellies filling the shelves from floor to ceiling...As Madam would say 'I have no fear of my own canning, but I'm always nervous of buying canned goods.'"

One of the earliest memories of her son, young George, was being taken by his mother when he was six years old to help her plant a maple sapling beside the veranda of the Annex. For the rest of his life that tree symbolized for him his mother's lasting imprint on the school. Sadly, no one noticed when this ancient tree was cut down in 1994 to make room for new construction.

In those years, the early part of the 20th century, most married women still hardly counted as independent beings. They couldn't even vote in Canada at the federal level until 1918. Being the wife of an energetic, dominant, totally engaged school principal would not have been easy for a proud or self-important person. But that was not Jessie. On the contrary, she loved the job.

Beyond her daily work in the school, she was involved in school social events and most formal ceremonies but usually in a quiet, supportive role. The Woollcombes of course were invited to Ottawa society events as a couple, "The Rev. and Mrs. G. P. Woollcombe", and the invitations arose from George's position. But Jessie was far from being shy and withdrawn in society. She was strong, practical, unselfish and gentle. She was well educated and had had a professional career of her own as a qualified teacher before she married George at the mature age of 35. She was the daughter of a large, successful and socially engaged family, the Mickles, with whom she remained in close touch. She was a leader in various ladies' charities, popular in those days, including the Women's Auxiliary of the Church of England and the Imperial Order of the Daughters of the Empire.

At home, Jessie was George Woollcombe's confidante, his advisor, the central pillar of his home life and the loving, competent mother of his children. He recognized this, but with typical English reserve. He seldom voiced his own emotions in any but the most restrained manner. His expression with her was full of gentle affection and humour. Two poems, written for his wife, illustrate this.

When the children were grown up he expressed, lovingly but rather formally, his deep appreciation for Jessie in a poem at a family Christmas party. Characteristically, he spoke more on behalf of the family members than for himself, as he praised their "Mother." The poem may say more about him than it does about her.

> *Christmas, tis said, is the Season for Youth,*
> *And in this there is doubtless a great deal of truth,*
> *But to-day from us all, Husband, Daughters and Sons,*

The Husbands of Daughters, and all other ones
The marks of affection that the Season calls forth
Are particularly centred on her whose true worth
We're unable to measure in mere human speech,
And yet we can say, though our aim we can't reach,
Our chief love and devotion, our best Christmas greeting
Are poured forth on her who is the soul of this Meeting.
To whom we owe that which we can ne'er hope to pay,
Who has unselfishly loved us and pointed the way
By example, by precept, mid storm and mid stress,
The way to true life and to real success,
Denying herself, her own pleasures, her health
She has given us a love above all earthly wealth,
A love that's begotten in Heaven alone
A love pure and Christ-like streaming right from God's throne,
And therefore today, with united accord
We greet her whom we know by that dear, sacred word
                    "Mother".

Then on Jessie's birthday in 1928, he accompanied his gift with this poem:

You have, I believe, had watches before,
And, to speak from mere memory, at least three or four.
But somehow or other they have always gone wrong,
Nor have you successfully kept them for long.
So on this day which we mark as the date of your birth,
And rejoice that God sent you to live upon earth,
To mark my affection and honour sublime,
I give you this watch which I know will keep time.
I trust it may prove a true help and a pleasure,
Both when you're at work and when you're at leisure!
And I hope it remains for a long time unbroken,
Of my love and devotion to have as a token.
                    G.P.Woollcombe

Memorial window in the chapel.

The schoolmaster

The G. P. Woollcombe memorial window in the Ashbury chapel symbolizes his life and his work. The three large lower panels illustrate him respectively as teacher, as spiritual leader, and as counsellor. He would not have separated these three facets; for him they were different aspects of the same job, to be a teacher of boys. This was the essence of his work and his ultimate aspiration. No doubt he was paternalistic, even by the standards of his day. But he was kind. He showed his fatherly concern for each individual boy under his care in a personal and direct manner. This concern affected his whole approach.

Woollcombe always remained in essence a teacher. Staying in direct touch with the classroom, the Head personally taught at least one class every week to each of the school's six 'Forms'. (Forms I to VI were roughly equivalent to Grades 2 through 12 today.) His subjects were classics (Greek and Latin), divinity and English. He also closely supervised the curriculum and the teaching of the other masters. He followed in detail each boy's progress in all subjects. Every Saturday he reviewed the weekly 'Form Reports' of all pupils, so that a boy who was weak in any particular subject might receive special attention.

Woollcombe's teaching methods were not innovative but conformed to the established conventions of the times. They were significantly influenced by his own English grammar school and Oxford education. His control of the class was total; his authority was never doubted or challenged behind his back. The directions in which he steered his pupils (as they were always called then, not 'students') were clear, reasonable and usually challenging. Much of his instruction did entail rote learning, which in those days was a generalized practice in schools.

His own classical academic background was reflected not only in his choice of subject matter but also in the examples he would choose to make a point. In class and in everyday informal conversation, he frequently cited Greek mythology or Latin phrases (e.g. *mutatis mutandi* or *miserabile visu*) or biblical adages (such as *Read, mark, learn and inwardly digest!*). He was stern, and would seldom tell jokes in class. But he was not feared so much as he was totally respected by the boys, and by most, in a distant, formal way, liked and admired.

The thoughtful educator.

G. P. Woollcombe's approach to education involved the whole person, not just the academic side of education. He had set out in clear terms Ashbury's formal, often repeated 'Object' (what we would now call its 'mission statement'). It became a mantra:

> To develop not only a high standard of scholarship, but also an upright, manly and Christian character in the boys entrusted to its care.

Good manners, respect for authority, consideration for others, chapel and religious instruction, not to mention regular team sports, were central. Even table manners: the school Calendar, an annual prospectus to advertise the school, noted in its 1929 version: "the resident Masters take their meals with the boys, and thus the important detail of correct deportment at table is not overlooked." In Ottawa society in those times, Woollcombe's approach was welcomed and promoted by Ashbury parents and supporters.

Of course discipline was an essential key to this approach. It meant in practice a system of prescribed punishments for various infractions of the rules and other misdemeanours. The rationale was that this should encourage good behaviour and help boys develop *self*-discipline. The Head was entirely in charge of this part of school life. It was he who set the rules and the tone, and it was mainly he who decided each case and administered the 'discipline'. Class masters could hand out milder punishments, such as writing out lines, or Saturday morning 'detentions' that were meted out in 15-minute 'quarters'. Boarders could also be 'gated' by the Housemaster.

Corporal punishment with rare exceptions was only given by the Head. But this was a very common experience for every boy who went to Ashbury throughout the Woollcombe years. The Head would call the young offender into his office and discuss the case sternly, but calmly and without the slightest anger. He would then administer the requisite punishment. This could be the strap on the hand for lesser offences, or so many strokes of the cane for more serious ones. For 'caning' he would use a flexible sergeant-major's swagger stick, not his solid walking stick, and there was never any question of the boys being required to pull their pants down.

In some ways the process was like that of a market place: One paid different prices for various behavioural offenses, comparable, one might say, to paying a parking ticket today. There was seldom resentment or anger involved on either side of the equation. Boys who had accumulated a number of 'quarters' of detention had the option of having them 'whacked off' by the Head on Saturday morning, paying what was considered the reasonable price – one stroke of the strap for each 'quarter'. In fact, to be given "six of the best" in a caning by the Head became a matter of pride for Ashbury boys, like a badge of honour. From all reports, there seldom ensued any lasting physical pain or serious psychological suffering. Boys later wryly recalled that the Head would precede his caning by saying, sincerely but a little self-righteously: "This will hurt me more than it hurts you". After it was over he would cite the Bible: "Go and sin no more."

Of course in all Canadian schools today, including Ashbury, corporal punishment is totally unacceptable, indeed illegal. Some explanation of the historical context is therefore needed. In those days this kind of discipline was seen by all not only as acceptable, but desirable. It was a selling point to prospective Ashbury parents who were pleased to have their boys come under the enlightened care of this highly regarded English school headmaster. To them, corporal punishment was an integral part of the system of education that the Rev. G. P. Woollcombe, M.A. (Oxon) was offering them, a system based on the much vaunted English public school model. Moreover, corporal punishment was universally practised throughout Canadian schools, both private and public.

By the 1920s the practice slowly started to be questioned in public opinion. For the first time in 1929, perhaps reacting to complaints he had heard, Woollcombe decided he needed to justify and clarify publicly his policy on the matter. So he put a note in that year's Ashbury College Calendar:

"No form of corporal punishment is given by the Masters or the Prefects. The Headmaster, and for House offences only, occasionally the Housemaster, alone administer this method of discipline, and then only when really advisable."

Public opinion on this subject continued to evolve. Many years after he retired, on the school's 50th anniversary in 1941, Woollcombe had a wide-ranging interview with *The Ottawa Journal*. Reflecting the changing attitudes toward the cane and the strap as punishment, the interviewer at one point asked him about this. His low-key response was qualified: "...the occasional licking [was] good for boys, but these practices had to be strictly regulated." The next day the sensationalist headline in the newspaper blared out: *"OCCASIONAL LICKING GOOD FOR BOYS SAYS ASHBURY COLLEGE FOUNDER!"* Indeed, times had changed since Woollcombe's day.

The overall picture one gets of G. P. Woollcombe in his relationship with Ashbury boys was of a teacher and headmaster who was firm and strict but kindly, and eminently fair. He dealt with each boy in an individual and personally concerned manner. No one questioned these qualities in him.

The last word we will leave to the boys he taught. In the late 1980s as Ashbury prepared a history of the school for its Centennial in 1991, a survey of opinions of many Ashbury alumni from the Woollcombe years was undertaken. In response to one of the questions "What did you know/think of the Headmaster?" these various, sometimes contradictory judgements constitute, when taken as a whole, a balanced retrospective of G. P. Woollcombe, the schoolmaster – "warts and all". Here is a selection of these opinions:

 – *Finest school head I ever ran into. Very stern, very fair. Gentle father figure especially for the younger boys. Poised. Unflappable. Caned frequently, but viewed it not with zeal but with a grudging sense of duty.*

– *Taught responsibility. Outstanding character builder. Backbone of Ashbury. He once gave me valuable sex lesson: "Beware of the girl with the sore on her lip."*

– *Fine, earnest man. Kindly martinet. Carried small cane. Gently tapped boys' shoulders in class. Latin tags: mirabile dictu. Discipline: 2, 4, or 6 cuts, lines or gating. No great academic pretensions.*

– *He would tap his fingertips together, and his sharp glistening eyes pierced you through wire-rimmed bifocals. He would then say "Well, my boy..." Once after asking him permission for town leave, he said to me "I expect you need to buy a new tooth brush."*

– *Approachable. Boarders considered him very friendly. Visited each room with a word for everyone twice a week before lights out. He was the only one who administered the cane.*

– *Dr. Woollcombe WAS Ashbury! It was his creation, was shaped by him and reflected this long, after he had retired. Although he liked to appear as a stern authoritarian, he was kindly, had real understanding of boys and an interest in individuals. In my case, and I believe it to be true of staff and students, he was respected and regarded with great affection. He had incredible energy and the quick darting movements of a bird. In fact, he resembled an emaciated eagle with a bald head and a scrawny neck encased in a Roman collar several sizes too large.*

– *Excellent guiding spirit.*

– *Really kind, understanding man who could read his pupils. Excellent teacher. He communicated.*

– *Stern but fair. Great stress on academic excellence and effort.*

– *Rather remote. Stern, strong discipline but never punished unduly.*

– *Taught religion and prepared some for confirmation. Voluminous robes. Carried gold pocket watch which was hard to retrieve; so boys often asked him the time!*

With all his students. June 1925.

The Englishman

In so many ways, G. P. Woollcombe remained thoroughly English while making his entire life's work in Canada. As we have seen, from the beginning he never considered Canada to be a foreign country. For him, in those days, it was essentially an extension of Britain. Aside from the climate and some cultural limitations, living in Canada did not entail a major change of life-style from that in England. His life at work was that of an English headmaster heading a school that he built up and ran on the English Public School model.

Similarly, Woollcombe's life at home, his relationships with family and friends and his use of leisure time, this all flowed directly from his English family upbringing and his education at Royal Grammar School and Oxford. There were no other major cultural influences in his formative years. His home life was conventional, without notable idiosyncrasies. He loved reading - both the ancient classics and novelists such as Dickens and Thomas Hardy, who to him were modern. On holidays or on board ship he would read paperback novels, which amused some in the family as being rather "racy" for this serious man. His favourite magazine was *Punch*, also known as *The London Charivari* and he would receive it every week from England. He would sometimes repeat quaint jokes from *Punch* to the family.

Music was not central in his personal habits although he did ensure it was an important part of Ashbury school life, mainly through the teaching and influence of J. Edgar Birch, the pioneering Ottawa musician. Birch, also an Englishman and the same age as GPW, had been a fellow teacher at Trinity College School in 1890-91. He and his wife and his two daughters became close family friends of the Woollcombes over many years together in Ottawa.

Out walking with his airedale "Fouce".

His afternoon tea, usually with one biscuit, was a regular ritual. His favourite hard candies were English humbugs. Sunday dinner, taken at mid-day, was a formal occasion. Sitting the head of the table, he would solemnly say grace before the family was allowed to lift their knives and forks. The main course was usually roast beef ("not rare, please"). He seldom smoked a cigarette, although occasionally a pipe. He sometimes indulged in one glass of sherry or brandy at family gatherings.

He loved animals and always had a large dog in his home as a pet. In the early evening he could be seen out walking his dog on the Ashbury grounds. Except on holiday, he dressed formally and seldom took off his clerical collar. As noted previously he stayed in close touch with his family in England by frequent letters and visited them in the summer.

On board ship to England

The English Public School model was marked by certain well-established features. These included strict discipline with well-known, traditional rules; an emphasis on classics in the curriculum; close connection with the Church of England; team sports; the organization of students into 'houses'; student prefects; the emphasis more on the boarding than the day school; and, of course, no question of having girls in these schools: they were only for boys. The Public Schools in England had roots going back many centuries, but in the early 19th century, one man, Thomas Arnold, the famous headmaster of Rugby School, led an historic reform based essentially on three principles: religious and moral rectitude, gentlemanly conduct, and academic performance. Virtually all the other English public and grammar schools followed suit in varying degrees. This, then, was the model that Woollcombe, himself a product of that system, brought to Ottawa.

Some of the more superficial habits imported from England were the school uniforms, masters wearing black academic gowns, and various terms which to our ears today sound archaic and quaint ('pupils', 'masters', 'prep', 'tuck shop', etc.). On formal occasions, the headmaster always wore his mortarboard cap of the style that signified a holder of a master's degree from Oxford. However the most salient English feature of G.P. Woollcombe's school was his choice of teaching staff. A review of staff lists shows that he almost always hired Englishmen to teach academic subjects. They were graduates of academically prestigious British universities, usually Oxford or Cambridge, with a preference for Oxford. The tone and accent in Ashbury classrooms, like that in many other private schools in Canada, was decidedly English.

Woollcombe nurtured his active network of connections in England, and would often decide on the hiring of masters during his summer trips there. He also regularly used 'Gabbitas and Thring', the London employment agency specializing in schoolmaster placement. The turnover of these English masters was disappointingly frequent, often after one or two years. This was sometimes due to the low salaries or other hardships of Ottawa life. Sometimes they did not live up to the Head's standards and he had to let them go.

With his Ashbury masters. 1926.

It should be noted in passing that some team sports played at Ashbury were authentically Canadian: particularly Canadian football in autumn and hockey in winter, although cricket was played in the spring. This conformed to the practice of other private schools with whom Ashbury usually competed, such as Lower Canada College in Montreal, St. Alban's in Brockville, and Bishop's College School in Lennoxville, Quebec.

Ashbury's close relationship with Rideau Hall during Woollcombe's years as headmaster years was reinforced by his own personal identification with Britain. Canada was still in the early stages of its evolution from a British colony to a self-governing Dominion. The Governor General, always an Englishman, represented the Queen or the King of England.

The Statute of Westminster in 1931 signaled an historic changed in that practice: Subsequent appointments were made by the "Monarch of Canada" and were on the advice of the Canadian Prime Minister, no longer the British Government. Finally in 1952 a Canadian, Vincent Massey, was appointed as Governor General. However, this was long after Woollcombe's day.

Several of the Governors General in the first half of the 20th century took an active personal interest in Ashbury College and its headmaster. The relationship was facilitated by the school's physical proximity once Ashbury had moved to Rockcliffe. Viceregal visits to the school were frequent, and the Woollcombes as well as Ashbury staff and boys were often invited to social functions at Rideau Hall. Two Governors Generals, Minto (1893-1904) and Devonshire (1916-1921), enrolled their sons in the school. Another, the Duke of Connaught (1911-1916), a son of Queen Victoria no less, was particularly involved with Ashbury. Many years later, in 1935, one of two school houses was named "Connaught" after him. The other house created at the same time was "Woollcombe". GPW had resigned two years previously. Incidentally Lord Alexander, Governor General from 1946 to 1952, also sent his two sons to Ashbury and a third house was given his name when he left Rideau Hall.

The Great War of 1914-1918 was one time in Canada's history when most Anglophone Canadians felt themselves to be very close to Britain in their hearts. Whatever the rights or the wrongs or the complexities of this war, which now a full century later we can put into perspective, and many now seriously criticize, in English Canada at that time, it wasn't complicated. There was no hesitation by the mass of the population to thrust themselves mind, body and spirit into battle beside the British and against "the Hun".

For Woollcombe, English to his core, these feelings were even more intense, dramatic, and traumatic than for many others. At 47, he was too old himself to enlist. In any event his duty, as he saw it, was to prepare his Ashbury boys to go to war beside England. Within the school, from

September 1914 on, all thoughts and prayers concerned the war. For the past few years, the Ashbury College Army Cadet Corps, associated with the Governor General's Foot Guards, had already been practicing for battle. All boys wanted to show their eagerness to finish school and join the war effort. If they didn't enlist right away, Woollcombe steered his graduating students towards Royal Military College, Kingston, or the Royal Naval College, Halifax.

By the end of the war, two thirds of all the Ashbury alumni, 282 out of 453, had gone to war, including the Head's oldest son, Philip, who enlisted as soon as he was old enough. This was in the context of a massive Canadian contribution, whereby 600,000 went to war out of a total population in 1918 of 8.3 million. Thirty-nine Ashburians were killed in World War I were killed in World War I and eighty wounded or invalided.

Woollcombe had personally seen to the education and care of each one of those boys. They had all been touched by his values of loyalty, honour, and duty. He spoke about them and prayed for them everyday in school's chapel services. Sometimes in the evening, he would go alone to pray in the chapel, after 'doing his rounds' of the boarders' dormitories.

One such evening that most faithful Ashbury factotum, Fred Oliver, was with him. Oliver later recalled that, as they went together into the chapel, the Head said,

> *"Oliver, bad news is beginning to reach us now. Casualties are always the outcome of war and there will be lots more to come before it's over. Such news I have received today....one of my boys. Come, we will kneel and ask God to comfort those who are left to mourn. For my boys I mourn also."*

Apart from their families, no one felt the losses more grievously than Woollcombe.

However traumatic were these years, nothing about the Great War would drastically change G. P. Woollcombe's basic world outlook, which had essentially been given shape in Oxford. He continued to look at current events and international developments in a very English way.

For example, he never doubted that the British Empire was essentially an extension of England. Loyalty to the British Monarchy was a matter of high principle, almost akin to belief in the Christian God. These were never questioned in his mind.

Woollcombe's outlook was not at all unusual. In his day most English-speaking Canadians, with the possible exception of the Irish, shared his views. He was more English than most within the Canadian society he worked and lived in, but in that era, this was seen as an attraction, as an advantage in his job as school principal. The waves of anti-colonialism, secularism and internationalism in the second half of the 20th century that would wash over Europe and North America (not to mention Asia and Africa) had not yet been felt. At the time of G. P. Woollcombe and early Ashbury College, these social revolutions were hardly even imagined. Moreover, any Canadian revolutionary attitudes were largely softened by Canada's slow but and steady, evolutionary growth of self-government and by its very gradual weaning away from the 'mother country'. Canadians were acutely conscious and very proud of this difference from United States, which defined Canada.

What is the historical significance of G. P. Woollcombe's 'Englishness'? It is true that the English in Canada at that time, as now, were just one strand of several that constituted the Canadian mosaic. Among the early settlers equally important were the French, the Scots, the Irish, and other Europeans, not to mention the aboriginal peoples. However, in the early 20th century, the British, including Scots and Irish as well as English, were dominant in terms of numbers: According to the 1911 census, 54 percent of the total population of 7.2 million were of British descent, and more than 10 percent were born in the British Isles. Moreover, to understand Canada, we must acknowledge that the British, for better or for worse, ruled this country for more than a century. They gave us the English language, our type of government and much of our legal system. Furthermore, in G. P. Woollcombe's life-time the English educational system, adapted to the Canadian context, was largely seen as a valuable model for the new Dominion to follow. And GPW was above all else an educator.

So, paradoxically, in his time Woollcombe the Englishman was quintessentially Canadian. His story is a reflection of Canada's story.

GPW and the Board

Throughout his time as Ashbury's headmaster, G. P. Woollcombe's relationship with his board of directors was vital and symbiotic. In essence, the directors assumed ultimate responsibility for the financial health of the school, and in fact were the main financial supporters, while leaving education policy decisions, as well as school administration, entirely to Woollcombe. Underlying this relationship from the beginning was an implicit social contract. The directors would keep the school financially afloat in return for Woollcombe providing their sons with what they considered the very best education available. Woollcombe never lost their confidence in this regard.

As we have seen, he was a strong-minded headmaster in full control of the school. Even on financial matters typically the board's actions and decisions were initiated by Woollcombe. He would set the fees and would propose new expenditures. He was the school's most active, and often its only fundraiser, which of course consumed much of his time and energy. Moreover, from the beginning the headmaster assumed the formal role and title of Secretary-Treasurer of the board. This gave him an additional measure of control.

A key to Woollcombe's productive relationship with the board was the close rapport, sometimes personal friendship, which he always nurtured with the board's president and with two or three other directors. This inner circle became the *de facto* executive committee. The members usually stayed involved for many years. Ashbury's first president, W. H. Rowley led the board from Ashbury's Wellington Street days until he died in 1915; legal advisor J. F. Orde stayed 21 years until he was appointed judge on the Supreme Court of Ontario and moved to Toronto; industrialist James W. Woods joined Rowley, Orde and Woollcombe in 1906 and then succeeded Rowley as president in 1915 until he, in turn, retired in 1931; magnate J. B. Fraser, Ashbury's most generous donor, joined the board in time to help finance the big move to Rockcliffe in 1910 and finally stood down in 1928. And there were a few others, including E. F. "Nixie" Newcombe. In 1919 Newcombe was the first 'old boy' (alumnus) to join the board. He took over as legal advisor from Orde in 1920. Over the following years he became an especially close friend of the Head, and during much of the 1920s they managed most of the school's business together as a team. (One year after G.P. retired in 1933, Newcombe took over as board president where he stayed, except for a brief pause, until 1949, dealing for better or for worse, with three Woollcombe successors.)

While the directors almost always took the headmaster's lead, this was not always the case. On a few issues it was the Board who ultimately won the day. We recall how in 1909, to the board's great distress, Woollcombe announced his resignation and imminent move to Bishop's College School, but how, faced with major resistance from the board, as well as from others, Woollcombe changed his mind.

In 1914 another fundamental difference emerged over the type of school Ashbury should be: boarding only, or mixed day-school and boarding. From the beginning Woollcombe had proclaimed that his vision for his school was to be essentially or even exclusively a boarding school. Although he had been a day-boy himself in a mixed boarding-day school in England, he was unshakably convinced that an entirely residential school was best for a boy's education. The famous English Public School model as well as his own experience in Canada with BCS and TCS had strengthened this conviction. The three moves Ashbury had made, to 188 Wellington in 1894, to Argyle Avenue in 1900 and to Rockcliffe in 1910 had all been mainly motivated by GPW's desire to bring in more boarders.

A strong-minded headmaster.

In the years following the Rockcliffe move with all its building costs, Ashbury was in serious financial difficulties. Moreover, there were not enough boarders enrolled to fill all the rooms available for them. Woollcombe's response to this problem was logical, determined and stubborn: since day-boys took as much classroom space as boarders at a fraction of the fees, from now on Ashbury should accept only boarders.

In the summer of 1914 he initially succeeded in persuading the reluctant board to go along with this. Woollcombe then rushed to announce the decision to the press.

PUPILS AT ASHBURY COLLEGE MUST RESIDE THERE IN THE FUTURE

At the annual meeting of the Ashbury College Board, held recently, it was decided that in the future all pupils attending the College must be in residence, which would consequently mean that no "day boys" would be allowed to attend.

This is an extremely important step and it is anticipated will have good results. The number of pupils will be reduced to about sixty, yet the board felt that they being all residents at the College will do away with all irregularities of attendance, the influence of outside distractions, etc.

Notice in The Ottawa Journal, July 9, 1914.

This ignited a general uproar over the summer on the part of day-boys' parents, whose deep pockets had mainly sustained the school from the beginning. By September 1, the board reversed its earlier decision and over-ruled Woollcombe's desires. Day-boys could return to the school at the discretion of the Head, but their fees would be raised substantially. This was the only time that Woollcombe was outrightly defeated by the board.

However, a short time later, the board decided on a major change in the school's constitution that arose not from the headmaster's initiative but from directors' concerns about chronically inadequate revenue. The move to Rockcliffe had entailed huge costs for the land purchase and the construction. This had been financed with heavy borrowing and the sale of new preferential shares. Nonetheless, it soon became evident, despite Woollcombe's continuous and assiduous fundraising efforts, that Ashbury was in over its head. It could not even pay interest on its creditors' loans, let alone issue any dividends on shares. Structural change was needed.

The pressure on the board to restructure came not from Woollcombe but starting in 1910 from J. B. Fraser, Ashbury's biggest financial supporter and creditor. He proposed transforming the school from a corporation owned by its shareholders to an educational foundation. Fraser had just observed a similar process successfully undertaken with St. Andrew's College, north of Toronto. Other directors agreed with him.

Woollcombe was slow in accepting that the economics had changed and that the days of the entrepreneur-principal had long since passed, but in the end he had to go along. Indeed, it was he who took on almost single-handedly the sad and delicate task of canvassing scores of Ashbury supporters to voluntarily surrender their shares and debentures. In return they received a voice in the management of the new corporation that was commensurate with the value of their surrendered holdings. These erstwhile shareholders were further enticed and flattered by being designated, confusingly and euphemistically, as "founders". When the new entity was formally established in June 1918, the directors became 'Governors'. This was arguably the most significant decision made by the board during Woollcombe's Rockcliffe years. It also pointed up the difference between the respective roles of the directors and the headmaster.

For G. P. Woollcombe's personal situation, this change was dramatic, both emotionally and financially. After starting out as the sole owner of his school and then for many years a significant shareholder, he suddenly had to say goodbye to his own substantial and hard-earned equity, while at the same time encouraging others to follow suit. While he had never received any dividends on his investment, the Rockcliffe campus was valuable land with a magnificent building. He must have envisaged ultimately selling out to a worthy successor on his retirement, which would bring him and Jessie a comfortable pension. Now with the new regime, more than ever he was an employee of the Board.

His own salary, negotiated discreetly with the wealthy inner circle of his board was never an issue, even though it was modest when compared with those of other school principals and with his impressive achievements and heavy responsibilities. It had been $1500 annually between 1908 and 1911 and then gradually raised to $2500 in 1915, where it now stood in 1918. He was from a modestly-off, well educated clerical background, but since his days at Christ Church, Oxford, he had always mingled with and worked closely with persons more prosperous than he. He was a respected, old-fashioned, well-educated schoolmaster and clergyman; they, in contrast, were industrialists and successful businessmen. They were so different, and yet in his case, the 'twain' did meet. He was conscious of this cultural difference and showed no resentment or arrogance with it. The only personal grievance Woollcombe later had with the board was their failure to provide an adequate pension for his retirement years.

Despite the major change in Ashbury's constitution in 1918, G. P. Woollcombe's eminence, his stature with the board and the broader Ashbury community was in no way diminished. He was still in charge of his school, and thus remained in control of his own still unfolding destiny. And Ashbury's finances now stood on more solid ground.

The Empire, the King, the Bible, and Christian morality

On Sunday morning, July 7, 1929 GPW found himself preaching to an Anglican congregation in Winnipeg. (Why he was there at that time will be explained further on.) His sermon was reported the next day in full and almost verbatim in *The Winnipeg Tribune*. He was inspired by the recent news of King George V's recovery from a near-death illness. Reproduced below is the entire newspaper story.

The sermon gives a striking picture of Woollcombe's views about the Empire, the King, and Christian morality. To our 21ˢᵗ century minds, some of these opinions are completely out-of-date, even shocking. Still, the fact the sermon was fully reported by Winnipeg's principal newspaper in an admiring manner suggests he was articulating common opinions and aspirations of the times. He used glowing biblical, monarchist and imperialist terms that were familiar to, and largely shared by, his audience. He was expressing the *zeitgeist*.

By today's standards G. P. Woollcombe was distinctly conservative in his social outlook. The religious and political views reflected in this sermon were broadly held by Woollcombe from his early education. He must have been sensitive to changing conditions and attitudes in Canada and Britain. But he died just before the transformative geopolitical and societal changes of the post-war era.

Nonetheless, were he alive today, he would argue that the essence of his message is as relevant now as it was in 1929, namely the importance of perseverance, patience and prayer. Whether others agreed or not, for him the primary objective of life was, as he put it, the giving of oneself to the service of God and one's fellows for the betterment of mankind. This was the dominant thread running through all his words and actions. The Winnipeg sermon sums it up nicely.

This, then, is from *The Winnipeg Tribune*, Monday, July 8, 1929, page 4:

HISTORY REPEATS ITSELF IN ILLNESS OF KING GEORGE V

REV. DR. G. P. WOOLLCOMBE FINDS HISTORIC
PARALLEL IN STORY OF HEZEKIAH'S HEALING

High tribute to His Majesty King George V as a great and good king, devoted to the service of his people and greatly beloved by them, was paid by Dr. G. P. Woollcombe in a sermon at St. Luke's church Sunday morning, at a service of thanksgiving for His Majesty's recovery.

Dr. Woollcombe, who is headmaster of Ashbury College, Ottawa, commenced a month's ministry at St. Luke's, Sunday. A special order of service with appropriate prayers and a special collect issued by His Grace Archbishop Matheson was used at the Thanksgiving service, and a choral celebration of Holy Communion was held.

Dr. Woollcombe based his sermon on the story of the healing of King Hezekiah recorded in the second book of Kings, chapter 20.

He told his congregation that the prayers of the people of Judah on behalf of Hezekiah, who lay at the point of death, were answered and the king restored to health. He had been a great king, and had done what was right in the sight of the Lord, he said.

The King's Illness

Many generations had passed away since the time of Hezekiah. Far-reaching changes had been written on the pages of the world's history. "Again we see a great and good king lying on what was feared would be his death-bed," said Dr. Woollcombe. "A king who feared God and used his influence to lead his people upwards and towards God's ideal for their true happiness.

"A king who devotedly sacrifices his own personal interests and pleasure to the welfare of his subjects. A king, too, who had helped most efficiently to pilot his people through the most severe and dangerous crisis in their history. A king who ruled, not over a small nation, but over the greatest and most magnificent Empire the world has ever known, and whose subjects are reckoned in hundreds of millions."

Dr. Woollcombe told of the wave of sorrow by which the Empire was swept when hope for the king's recovery was dim. He spoke of the prayers for his recovery "poured forth from practically every place of worship throughout the Empire, and from millions of individual hearts.

Sound of Thanksgiving

He referred to the wealth of joy which moved the hearts of his people when His Majesty began to make progress toward recovery.

"So today throughout the length and breadth of our great Empire," said the preacher, "there is being sounded a note of solemn, yet joyful thanksgiving to Almighty God for giving us back our well-beloved King, and we join with our thanksgiving the earnest wish that our most gracious Sovereign Lord King George may be spared to continue for many years as the head of our great Empire, and as our devoted leader and friend."

There were three things that stood out prominently in connection with the King's late illness. One was his patience under great weakness and suffering. Another was his perseverance and his will to live. The other was the atmosphere of prayer that filled, not only his sick chamber, but also his whole Empire.

These were factors of no small importance among the means, which, under God, were successful in bringing back His Majesty from the gates of death.

Sacrifice Needed

Dr. Woollcombe told his hearers that their thanksgiving should be more than merely joining in prayers, singing stirring hymns, or listening to patriotic discourses.

In the Bible, national thanksgiving was always associated with sacrifice. True sacrifice was the giving of that which cost something. The greatest sacrifice was that of giving themselves to the service of God and their fellows.

In striving to associate their thanksgiving with sacrifice they could not do better than cultivate patience, perseverance and prayer.

Dr. Woollcombe first stressed the need of making these characteristics prominent in connection with their thought of Empire. They should exercise patience with reference to the problems that had to be solved, and towards the various governments of the Empire, whose difficulties it was often hard for them to realize.

In times of peace they should exercise the same patience by which they were characterized in the dark days of the Great War.

Perseverance was also necessary. They should continue to keep in mind the great purpose of the Empire.

Empire Task

This was not to be interpreted in terms of its vast extent, its wealth, and resources, but in terms of its task, the betterment of mankind at large.

They also needed to pray that the Empire might continue to be really great. Prayer implied dependence on God. It involved recognition that their destinies were in His hands, and that unless as an Empire they followed after righteousness they could not hope to continue as his instrument for bringing about His world-wide purposes.

The same three characteristics were needed in their national outlook. Patience was necessary. They needed to realize that great things could not be accomplished in a moment. "It is better even for our population to increase slowly than for it to be artificially inflated with undesirable citizens," the preacher said.

Their vast resources also should be developed normally rather than with an undue stimulus.

Need of Determination

Necessary also was the spirit of perseverance. "We need to meet and overcome all the difficulties inherent in our national life with the spirit of determination to go on whatever obstacles may lie in our paths," he said.

With regard to prayer – the nation could not become really great nor exercise a world-wide influence for good unless she recognized her dependence on Almighty God, and sought to do His will.

In conclusion, Dr. Woollcombe stressed the need of patience, perseverance and prayer in individual life. "What its citizens are in their private lives, the nation will inevitably tend to become," he said.

Family life would be greatened and troubles avoided if they were patient with the words and actions of one another. Paul's advice to be patient to all men, should be followed. Perseverance also was essential whatever their calling in life.

Prayer, too. The only effectual way in which they could offer themselves as a real sacrifice and thus help make their country truly great was by cultivating a personal atmosphere of prayer.

Sunny years at Ashbury

In September 1923 George and Jessie Woollcombe left the rented house on Cloverdale Avenue and moved into their brand new home, called the Headmaster's House. The school had built for their headmaster a large, handsome modern brick house, amply suited for all their needs and desires and perfectly located only a few yards from the school's front door. They would live there for their last decade with Ashbury College. This has remained the home of the school's headmasters ever since.

Things were going well in their lives at that time. These were good years. There was reason for them to be gratified both with the state of school and with their own close family. And they remained confidently optimistic for a few more years to come.

Since the serious financial problems of previous years and the ensuing radical changes in Ashbury's ownership and legal structure in 1918, the dark clouds had dispersed. The lean years seemed to be over. From 1919 on, enrolment was full. With at least 74 boarders, which was the maximum number the Rockcliffe building and staff could easily handle, plus about 35 day-boys, the school was showing a healthy profit. GPW, that great advocate of boarding schools, could believe he had won the day. Since Argyle days, when Ashbury was an Ottawa day school with a few boarders, it had become a Rockcliffe boarding school with a minority of day-boys. About one third of the students were from Montreal, thanks to the Head's continuous, active promotion there; one third were from other parts of Canada; and the remainder were mainly from wealthy, established old Ottawa families, senior civil servants and transient parliamentarians.

The new Headmaster's House, 1923.

On the academic side, Ashbury's reputation in Canada was becoming stronger, as alumni showed up well in universities, notably McGill, and the Royal Military College. With the war years over, Woollcombe had been able to recruit several good masters on his summer trips. Harry Wright, judged by all to be an excellent maths and science teacher, joined the school in 1919. In 1923 G.P. made him deputy headmaster. He later became Woollcombe's successor as headmaster. W.H. "Steve" Brodie, a scholarly veteran of WWI battles in Gallipoli and Mesopotamia, joined the staff in 1922. He revived theatre arts in Ashbury, directing Shakespeare productions annually. He also taught French – as if it were a dead language. (Alas, this was in keeping with the times.) Nonetheless G.P. regarded Brodie highly and in 1923 appointed him housemaster in charge of boarding life. The following summer he was pleased when Brodie asked for his eldest daughter Maithol's hand in marriage.

Substantial physical evidence of Ashbury's rising star in the 1920s was the new 'Memorial Wing', in honour of Ashburians killed in the Great War. Formally opened by the Governor General, Lord Byng, on June 11, 1924, it comprised a large gymnasium (at least considered large in those days), boarders' and masters' bedrooms, a classroom for the senior form, science labs, a locker room and showers, a rifle range and a large modern coal furnace which gave central heating for the whole school as well as the headmaster's house. This had been entirely Woollcombe's concept and initiative. To make it happen he had undertaken another of his marathon singlehanded fund-raising campaigns, aiming to raise $60,000. When the returns were very slow, he unhesitatingly harassed alumni for over three years, but the board still needed to take out a $30,000 mortgage to cover the shortfall.

Nevertheless, the school had operating surpluses for most of the twenties and was doing well. Woollcombe was the catalyst for this success, and in 1920 the board doubled his annual salary from $2500 in 1918 to $4800, plus housing, plus a $500 'bonus' each year. In 1925 and again in 1926, he was given an additional 'extraordinary bonus' of $500.

In Woollcombe's mind perhaps the most gratifying recognition came in 1926, when McGill University conferred an honorary doctorate on him. The annual convocation was a solemn ceremony held at noon on May 27, in Montreal's grand and massive, old Capitol Theatre on Ste. Catherine Street. It was presided over by the Principal and Vice-Chancellor, General Sir Arthur Currie in front of more than 2000 graduating students, faculty, various dignitaries and well-wishers. Before the scarlet and white hood of a Doctor of Laws was placed over his shoulders, Woollcombe was presented to the Vice-Chancellor with the following testimony:

> *Mr. Vice-Chancellor, I have the honour to present to you that you may confer on him the degree of Doctor of Laws, honoris causis, George P. Woollcombe, Headmaster, Ashbury College, Ottawa, Honours Graduate of Oxford University; staunch standard bearer of education; eminent member of a long and honourable line of school principals, who long ago perceived the educational needs of Canada and used his capacity to make his vision true; for more than thirty-five years devoted to the educational services of his adopted country; worthy head of a school national in its scope, great in its service to our Dominion, and allied to us at McGill by the giving to us yearly of its many sons; an enthusiastic counsellor of youth whose breadth of outlook and richness of sympathy has won him the esteem and confidence of the men to whom in boyhood he was a kindly guide and a steadfast friend.*

These words summed up what had been G.P. Woollcombe's personal aspiration in the cause of educating future generations.

Important to note, the new degree also brought him the significant advantage of allowing him forever thereafter to call himself "Dr. Woollcombe". He may have smiled with satisfaction to himself: "This is a nice addition to my public persona !"

Woollcombe's life outside of school affairs continued apace throughout the 1920s. He took full advantage of his vacations, sojourning usually with Jessie and often with friends, in holiday retreats in the Eastern Townships, New Brunswick, the eastern seaboard of the US, even once on a Caribbean cruise and once to Majorca. And of course his summer trip to England, usually without Jessie, was his sacred annual respite. Since he went to recruit teachers as well as see his family, the Ashbury board often authorized his passage to be paid by the school. During the war years he did not travel abroad.

On January 1919, just two months after the Armistice, he wrote an affectionate letter to his son, who was about to sail for England. This letter says a lot about his feelings towards family, his friends and 'his boys' at Ashbury, his desire to revisit England, as well as his habits of thought and speech.

My dear Philip,

Very many thanks for your letter.....So many thanks, old man, for the $20. I will put it away and keep it for the summer when I hope to see you in England....I am sending this to Olympic [no doubt, the name of Philip's ship] *in the hopes of it reaching you before she sails. Mr. Orde* [his grand old friend, the Ashbury lawyer] *has just sent me the enclosed note regarding a friend of his in Wales. If you get a chance look her up as Mr. Orde says she is anxious to entertain Canadian officers....*

We have had about 15 boys down with the Flu! [the Spanish flu epidemic] *and we have consequentially been very busy, not to say anxious. All now are on the mend, and I hope we shall not have many more cases – Parents get so nervous!*

I hope you will have a very nice voyage and not be sick. I wish I were going with you. I yearn for the sea air and to 'pace the deck' after nearly five years....

With every good wish and love to all the people at home. ["people at home" of course were his family in England]

> *I am*
> *Yr always affectionate Father*
> *Geo. P. Woollcombe*

Also in other respects the 1920s were good years. By the end of the Great War, Jessie had given up her full-time work supervising all the school's housekeeping affairs. She now became the "Honorary Housekeeper" advising on domestic arrangements. The five children were now grownup and she was able to devote more of her time to her church work, her charities, literary groups, and the I.O.D.E., of which she was educational secretary for the Ottawa branch.

George and Jessie were satisfied with how their children had turned out. Philip the oldest, had enlisted as a private in the army as soon as the war started and went to the Front. He was quickly promoted up through the ranks to sergeant, lieutenant, and finally captain. He stayed on for a while overseas after the war, working in England and then returned to Canada in 1924, settling in Montreal, employed by Dominion Engineering. His home there became the primary Montreal base for the rest of his father's life. G.P. Woollcombe visited that city constantly. In 1932 Philip joined the Cadbury chocolate company as sales manager, and then married Shirley Stiles, in the Ashbury chapel.

The two daughters, Maithol and Phyllis, continued living at the Headmaster's House until their weddings both in June 1925, six days apart. Both were married by their father in the Ashbury chapel. As mentioned, Maithol married Ashbury teacher "Steve" Brodie and they had two sons while living at the school. In 1937, Brodie had serious professional differences with the new headmaster (GPW's second successor, Archdale) and took a senior job with the CBC. Their Toronto home then naturally became the main base in that city for all the Woollcombe family.

Phyllis married Dr. Wakely Abbott-Smith, a Montreal physician and decorated war veteran, the son of an Anglican clergyman and classics scholar at McGill. This seemed to be a perfect match. The marriage, alas, was short and unhappy. She did bear the first Woollcombe grandchildren however – Kenneth in 1926 and John in 1928. They lived in Montreal but Phyllis, with her sons, frequently visited her parents in Ottawa. The Abbott-Smiths spent a year in Vienna while Wakely pursued further medical studies. Soon after their return, on May 8, 1930, deeply depressed, Wakely ended his life suddenly in the basement of their Montreal home. Following this tragic shock, Phyllis, the beautiful young widow, lived permanently with her parents, wherever that would be. George and Jessie helped her raise the two boys and paid for their schooling.

GPW's two younger boys, Jessie's sons, Edward and George, graduated from Ashbury in 1916 and 1920 respectively. Both attended the Royal Naval College of Canada, Edward when it was located in Halifax, where he witnessed the great Halifax harbour explosion in 1917, and in George's case after it moved to Esquimalt, B.C. Edward then took Engineering at McGill and went on to become head of Foundation Maritime Ltd., a major marine salvage firm in Halifax. In this capacity, he made a substantial contribution to the war effort during WW2 for which he was awarded the Order of the British Empire (OBE).

In the meantime, in 1930 Edward had married Lillian Baker in Christ Church Cathedral, Ottawa, with his father helping to officiate in the ceremony. Edward and Lillian's first child, Ted, was a babe in arms on a visit to the Headmaster's House in the spring of 1933

With their grandchildren, Spring 1933.

As for George junior, he graduated in Commerce from McGill in 1925, became a chartered accountant, and married the widow Dorothy Boehm Smart in 1934. Their second child, the youngest Woollcombe grandchild, is the author of this present biography.

Slowing down

However much G. P. Woollcombe may have been happy with his life in those years, by the time he was 60 in 1927, he was starting to slow down. He no longer kept up the same pace in his classroom teaching. He had become only an occasional replacement teacher for the other masters, as needed and whenever he chose to. He increasingly delegated some of his supervisory responsibilities, both to Harry Wright and to his son-in-law, Steve Brodie. He had appointed Brodie housemaster in

1923 at the same time as Wright became his deputy head. Then in 1931 he put Brodie in charge of the newly separated-off Junior School for boys aged eight to 12 or 13, with a staff of junior teachers under him. Although as late as June 1931, he boldly talked about his "hope that a separate building [for the Junior School] will be a reality in a short time", this was a dream which nobody on the board took very seriously.

By 1928, he had not yet decided when he would leave the school. At that year's Closing, the press reported him declaring "that the rumour was prevalent in Montreal that he was retiring from the headmastership forthwith, and he wished to deny it most emphatically as he expected to stay on for many more years if he was spared to do so." Apparently his ulterior motive was to squelch a rumour in order to not undermine an upcoming fundraising campaign. He had also implied to his friend and confidant, board member Nixie Newcombe, that he "could stay until he was 70".

However also in 1928, Woollcombe had broached the subject of a pension for his eventual retirement with the board. He suggested $4000 annually. There was much heated discussion of the subject, formally and informally, among the governors and for a long while nothing was done. The basic problem was the utter failure of fiduciary foresight on the part of the board of governors. As described in Tony German's 1991 history of the school: "The experienced board of very substantial businessmen in fact directed no accumulation for any purpose at all – nothing for depreciation, building replacement or expansion, scholarships or bursaries. Ashbury's business was very solidly attended day by day and year by year, but the future was blithely ignored." Notwithstanding, by early 1929 G.P. put a specific proposal to the board and was promised a "retirement allowance" of "not less than $3000 per year and $1000 for Mrs. Woollcombe should she survive him." Had this discussion happened a couple of years later, after the Great Depression had struck the world and Canada, the outcome would not have been so favourable.

In these years, Woollcombe's thoughts turned increasingly to the other great profession of his life, that of a clergyman. Later, as we shall see, he would go back to England as a country vicar, but for the time being he needed to stay in Canada. So, in 1929, having advised the board well in advance and having advanced his trip to England to late April, he took on an assignment in Manitoba for the month of July. During the absence of the regular rector he took charge of St. Luke's Church, Fort Rouge in central Winnipeg. He preached and took services, twice on Sundays. He and Jessie lived in the parish rectory. While in Manitoba, Woollcombe of course took every occasion to promote Ashbury College, notably to potential parents.

Another big personal advantage of this time away was that he and Jessie had the very rare opportunity to see his dear brother Lionel. Lionel had been together with George and Julia in Ottawa way back when Ashbury House School was just getting started on Wellington St. and he had been Best Man at George's wedding to Jessie in 1900. Then in 1904 Lionel had married a Manitoba girl, Ethel Pearce and settled with her in Rapid City, Manitoba. There he had become a bank manager and they had raised a family.

However, George apparently did not visit his wayward brother Willy, who at the time was out of touch, somewhere in Manitoba.

In early August George and Jessie took the long train journey back to Ottawa, thinking about future plans.

Saying farewell

G. P. Woollcombe understood that the time was approaching when he should move on. As described above, after many hard-working years, he had slowed down. He was simply unable to give his school the same drive and energy as in the past. Both he and his wife were having health problems as they grew older. His children were well into careers of their own. He had a realistic plan for a second career as a parish clergyman. Plus, he now had the formal promise of a retirement allowance in hand. Moreover, he had accomplished his most important goals: His little one room school in 1891 had grown to be one of the top boarding schools of Canada, its reputation and future growth seemingly assured. The values, the minds and the bodies of many hundreds of boys had been formed under his guidance. So clearly it now was time to say farewell.

All this would have set the perfect scene for a triumphal departure from Ashbury with optimism and an easy mind, except for one major worry. The Depression had struck with a vengeance, and Ashbury bore the full brunt of it. Gone were the days of operational surpluses and full enrolment. The number of students had been dropping since 1930, especially boarders. For 1933-34 the school had 45 day-boys and only 55 boarders, so there were 20 empty beds. Deficits followed one after another along with searches for new bank loans. Salaries were cut and staff were let go. There was not much optimism in the air.

Then in the spring of 1933, GPW was ill for several weeks, including a stay in the Presbyterian Hospital on the corner of Rideau and Charlotte Streets. As soon as he recovered and re-emerged, he asked to meet with the board of governors. On May 15, he tendered his resignation to take effect at the end of the school term in June. The board announced that they had "reluctantly accepted" it.

The Ottawa Journal interviewed Woollcombe that evening:

> *"he explained his resignation was due to his feeling that in the interests of the school, and of himself personally, the time has arrived when he should relinquish his duties to a younger and more vigorous man. Asked as to his future plans, Dr. Woollcombe said they were indefinite, but it was likely he would take over parish work for the Anglican Church either in England or in Canada. Dr. Woollcombe said he purposed taking his annual trip to England this summer."*

At the very same time, the board announced the appointment of Harry Wright as Woollcombe's successor. This was GPW's recommendation and, unsurprisingly, there was no one else was given consideration. Wright was warmly welcomed into the position by the governors and everyone else. For over 14 years at Ashbury he had made a strong name for himself as an excellent teacher. GPW publicly praised him and expressed full confidence that the past policies and traditions would be continued. Unfortunately, as it turned out, Wright did not work out well as headmaster. He did not show the requisite leadership, and within three years another successor to Woollcombe was being sought. Ironically, then, in 'his finest hour', history must record that Woollcombe's judgement failed him on the crucial matter of succession.

But for the moment it was G.P. Woollcombe's day of glory and honour, his last day in office. The Closing ceremonies were held under clear skies on the afternoon of Wednesday June 14th on the lawn in front of the school building. All the schoolboys and the staff sat in rows in front of the platform where the governors and other dignitaries were seated, surrounding G.P. and Mrs. Woollcombe. There were glowing words of appreciation and presentation of gifts to the retiring founder-headmaster and his wife. Then he stood up to speak. As he had done every June at the Closing ceremonies since the beginning, he first gave his customary report on all the various successes the school had achieved in the past year, his praise of particular staff members, the prefects, the sports teams, the school's financial benefactors, and so on.

He then turned to the matter that was on everybody's mind:

> "It is now almost 42 years since I founded the school which is therefore in a special sense my child. I have watched it grow, oftentimes amid great difficulties, from a very small beginning into the important educational institution that it is today. Hundreds of boys have passed through my hands and I am thankful and proud to state that the very great majority of them have developed into good and useful citizens of our Empire. This fact alone is more than compensation for the many years I have devoted to my work. It is necessarily a great and severe wrench for me to relinquish my post here and to say good-bye to Ashbury, but I have decided that it is best for me to do so, I expect in the near future to take up parish work either in England or in Canada. Wherever I may be, Ashbury will always have first place in my affections."

He expressed confidence in his successor, Mr. Wright, but his strongest praise was for Jessie Woollcombe, to whom he said much of Ashbury's success was owed. He declared "She has been a tower of strength to me for the past 33 years and her wise counsel and unselfish devotion to the interests of the boys were of inestimable value."

He ended his speech, inevitably, with some of his familiar high-minded moral advice:

> "My parting words to all connected with Ashbury, whether as past or as present pupils are: Be loyal to your school; play the game in the fullest sense of the term, and do your best to advance its true interests"

An editorial in *The Ottawa Citizen* that day was entitled:

'A CANADIAN SCHOOLMASTER'

> As headmaster for forty-two years, since he founded Ashbury College, Dr. G. P. Woollcombe has sure made a great contribution to education in in Canada. Everywhere throughout the country, as well as in distant lands, Dr. Woollcombe's former pupils are giving practical evidence of the value of the early training they received. They have taken with them into adult years Ashbury's spirit of fair play and diligence. Dr. Woollcombe's own high sense of justice and righteous living is reflected in Ashbury's fine reputation.

> The school itself in Rockcliffe is an enduring monument to its founder. It is the visible monument; but the lives of the men who have passed through the school bear witness even more substantially to Dr. Woollcombe's contribution to Canadian citizenship.

Within a few days the Woollcombes were well into the business of packing up all their memories along with their personal effects. They were moving on. By mid-July George was already in England preparing the ground for the next chapter of their lives. On July 31, Jessie joined him in London.

On retirement from Ashbury, 1933.

VI. The Last Chapters of his Life

Back to his roots

For long years previously Woollcombe had been imagining his life, post-Ashbury. As at previous critical turning points, he had a clear goal, and he set out in an unhesitating, determined way to define it more specifically and then to achieve it. At this stage of his life he knew that he wanted to go back to his roots. He envisioned being vicar of a country parish in central England, as his father before him.

In those days, however, most clergy appointments in the Church of England, similar to officer commissions in the Army, depended on one's connections – on whom one knew, on patronage. Moreover, under the Colonial Clergy Act of 1874, for those clergyman whose ordination and previous years of service had been in Canada, appointments in Britain required both the permission of the Archbishop of Canterbury as well as the nomination by the bishop of the would-be host diocese. And of course there needed to be an opening. So on the very day he submitted his resignation to the Ashbury board, Woollcombe wrote to his most influential friend in Britain for help. This was none other than Lord Byng, the former Governor General who was now retired and living on his estate in Essex. GPW explained his desire to establish himself in an English country vicarage. This high-level appeal paid off decisively and Byng responded immediately. On fine, pale blue notepaper in his aristocratic handwriting he wrote:

May 20th, 1933

My dear Headmaster,

Your letter reached me yesterday and I hasten to tell you how sorry I am to think of Ashbury running without your guiding hand and successful leadership.

*But perhaps you are right to leave when you can still take
up another office which I can only hope provide the same
happy associations that you must retain of Ashbury.*

*I am writing to the Lord Chancellor and enclosing your letter to me
which sets forth the case and its reasons far better than I can.*

I have no living in my gift, nor do I think that any of my nephews
(Stratford, Hylton and Normanton) have a vacancy at the
present time. So it would seem wiser to put the matter in the
hands of those who have a wider knowledge of the subject.*

With very warmest wishes from us both,

*Yrs sincerely
Byng of Vimy*

* Note that a "living" means an appointed position in the church, including the income
associated with it, and "in my gift" meant "within my power or right to give"

While neither Byng nor his noble nephews had any clergy vacancies to dispense, his passing on of Woollcombe's request to the Lord Chancellor bore fruit. The Lord Chancellor is a cabinet-level officer of state in the U.K. with various important official functions, including that of appointing "livings" to a few hundred parishes within the Established Church of England.

An ancient parish in central London was proposed, St. Mary's Stoke Newington. (This little church, built in 1563, is still functioning and claims to be the only surviving Elizabethan church in London.) It may also have been the Lord Chancellor who referred Woollcombe's request to the Archbishop of Canterbury, whose formal permission was then granted. GPW rented a small townhouse a few blocks away from this church, at 14 Kings Road. Then George, Jessie, Phyllis and the two young boys set up their temporary new home. For the first time in his life, he was given the job of running a parish.

However, an urban church was not what he had planned on. By early spring 1934 he learned that a country parish would be available for him. He jumped at the chance.

Back in Canada, a notice appearing in *The Ottawa Journal* would have interested Ottawa readers wondering what had happened to GPW:

> *London, March 29. Rev. G.P.Woollcombe, former headmaster of Ashbury College, at Ottawa, has been appointed vicar of Woodford Halse with Hinton and West Farndon, Rugby. The patron of the living, which is of the value of $1,600, is the Lord Chancellor.*

This information likely came directly from Woollcombe, who conveniently had translated pounds into equivalent Canadian dollars for the newspaper.

Woodford Halse was an ancient rural village in the English Midlands. It had a population of about 1800 at that time. Situated on the mainline of the Great Central Railway, it was about 60 miles north-east of London's Marylebone Station, a two-hour train journey away. The main economic activity was horticulture and the railway yard. Woollcombe was to be Vicar at St. Mary the Virgin, the only Anglican church in the village. Dating back to about 1300 AD, it was a fine, gothic stone and brick building. The nearby vicarage*, where the Woollcombe family would stay, was built somewhat more recently but of a similar style.

*The term "vicarage" applies both to the position and to the residence that goes with it.

It was several more months before they actually made the move. After securing formal approval from the Right Reverend Claude Blagden, Bishop of Peterborough, on September 24, 1934, GPW was solemnly inducted into the "Vicarage and Parish Church of Woodford Halse". In this ceremony, "George Penrose Woollcombe, the incumbent" was given his formal mandate. Thus licensed by the bishop, he made a "Declaration of Assent" (committing himself to doctrinal orthodoxy), and swore two oaths, that of Allegiance (to the King) and that of Canonical Obedience (to the Bishop). His mandate from the bishop stipulated he was to "admonish his people to bring their infant children to be baptized in a timely way, to preach God's Holy Word in two full services every Sunday, and to frequently celebrate the Holy Communion." After all that august formality, Bishop Blagden blessed the new vicar, and there was general celebration.

Church of St. Mary the Virgin, Woodford Halse.

Thus prepared, Woollcombe now set out with his chosen second career. As it turned out, however, his time at Woodford Halse would last less than three years. Initially everything seemed perfectly in line with his long-cherished hopes. This was just the kind of English country vicarage in which he had dreamed spending the autumn of his life. In his mind, there was no doubt that his values, his personal inclinations, his upbringing, his education and his culture eminently suited him for the clearly prescribed role the vicarage offered.

Unlike his first years in Canada nearly a half century previously, he was no longer driven by a young man's desire to change the world. But neither was he resting on his laurels: he had a serious challenge before him. He was politely welcomed by the parishioners, who were mainly families that had lived and worked and raised their children there for many generations. However, for them the new vicar was an outsider, perhaps even a foreigner. For Woollcombe this was a far cry from his recent triumphal departure from Ashbury.

The Vicar of Woodford Halse.

He quickly got started in his new job. He took services and preached twice every Sunday. During the week, he had pastoral care duties, dealing with parishioners' concerns as best he could. He endeavoured to become accepted as their pastor, as his father had been in Loudwater. Despite his church work in the past, however, much of it was quite new for him. More fundamentally, his basic identity had suddenly changed: He was no longer an educator in Canada; he was now an English country vicar.

On the other hand, while in England George had the satisfaction of being able to see his English siblings and their families more frequently. He was, after all, the patriarch of his close-knit family and had stayed in touch with them all while living in Canada, especially during his annual summer trips. Now, his connections with those in England were easier.

His older sister Daisy had married an Anglican cleric, now retired, and was living in Somerset in the southwest. His closest sister in age, Mabel, had died a few years previously but her daughter Doris was a special favourite and lived in Berkshire, just west of London. She was an intimate friend of her cousin, GPW's daughter, Phyllis. Madeline, who also had married a clergyman, was living in Sussex, in the south. Eleanor, the youngest sister, was unmarried and was a pharmacist in London. One other sister, Henrietta, or "Hetty" had moved to New Zealand with her husband, also a clergyman. Perhaps closest of all to GPW was his brother John, the Benjamin of the family. As noted earlier, John had come to teach for a couple of years at Ashbury when the school was on Argyle Avenue. On return to England he took Holy Orders, as had so many in the family. Now he was in fact Vicar of Loudwater, the very same parish his father had served for so long and where the siblings had all grown up. For sentimental reasons GPW might well have wished to have had that job himself, but it was not available! Still, Loudwater was not far, only some 50 miles away, and he loved to visit his brother, now living in the old family homestead.

Moreover, GPW could also easily drive to Oxford, which was even closer, about 30 miles distant. With his Oxonian M.A. he had the right to visit the Senior Common Room of his alma mater, Christ Church, and indulge in nostalgic recollection of his university days.

Meanwhile, on the home front, Jessie, Phyllis and the two grandsons tried to adjust to life in the vicarage. The house was adequate compared to some English rectories. It had room enough for all, including occasional visitors, and a live-in domestic servant called Mary. It also had lovely gardens all around where the ladies could stroll about and Phyllis' boys could play. But the house was so cold! How Jessie missed her home at Ashbury, with all its comforts, especially its central heating, a feature quite unknown in the English countryside. (It has been said that stern English schoolmasters equated being cold with strengthening a boy's moral fibre!) Jessie also missed her active social and intellectual life with her friends in Ottawa. George had a clearly defined job but Jessie no longer had responsibilities outside the home. Moreover, he was a Woollcombe and the Woollcombe family was distinctly English; she was a Mickle and the Mickles were Canadian.

The boys were a constant, but welcome challenge. At least in their first years in England, they were tutored at home by their grandparents. (Jessie of course had been a professional teacher before marrying George.) For their last two years in England, Kenneth and John Abbott-Smith were sent to boarding school.

But Jessie's life was far from dreary. George had bought a small car, which all three adults would drive regularly. There were many excursions through the lovely Midlands countryside, and to such nearby towns as Northampton and Banbury (of Banbury Cross fame) as well as Oxford and Loudwater. Jessie often took the train down to London for business or pleasure. When in London both she and George usually stayed at the posh Cumberland Hotel near Marble Arch. She would take holidays on her own when George could not leave his parish, sometimes to the coastal resort of Eastbourne.

While she missed her children and her Mickle family in Canada, she had great joy when both her own sons came to England, Edward in early 1935 for several weeks, and in February 1935 George Andrew came with his new bride Dorothy, for a full year. He was on assignment to London with his firm, Confederation Life. The next year, in the spring of 1937 George junior and Dorothy came back to England for a few months, this time with their infant daughter Jennifer. The senior Woollcombes engaged a nursemaid for that time so they could have their new granddaughter staying with them in Woodford Halse, while George and Dorothy visited the vicarage on weekends. While in England, Dorothy became truly like a daughter in Jessie's affections and they remained very close for the rest of Jessie's life.

Jessie and GPW with their granddaughter Jennifer.

Initially, the Woollcombes' household financial situation was adequate for their needs. He had the $3000 annual retirement allowance from Ashbury, plus the 'living' of $1600 per year that came with the vicarage. They had the additional expenses of supporting Phyllis and the two boys, but the cost of living was low, especially since this was the depth of the Great Depression. It may be that Britain suffered somewhat less than Canada and the U.S. "People in England are not talking about the Depression as much as we are here" had been

GPW's reassuring response to an enquiring journalist in August 1932 on returning to Canada from his summer visit. He explained that the English were "just tightening their belts and getting on with it, but they regarded the situation as more hopeful."

However, in February 1936, Woollcombe received an unwelcome letter. It was from the Ashbury board chairman, Nixie Newcombe, who had been GPW's closest colleague and an old friend. Newcombe now wrote to inform him that in view of the dire financial straits the school was in, his Ashbury pension was being cut by half, to $1500 a year. This seemed to be an outright breach of promise, and a hurtful one at that. The consequences of the Depression and questionable management at Ashbury after GPW had left had caught up with him. Woollcombe's financial situation had become precarious, and it was aggravated by the cost of sending his grandsons to boarding school.

In this situation, his various other concerns began to weigh more heavily on George's mind. There were Jessie's mixed feelings about living in Woodford Halse. There was the uncomfortable reality that in this traditional parish he was still seen as an outsider, despite his good work. When not listening to his better angels, George may have been tempted by the feeling that he was not nearly as important a figure in Woodford Halse as he had been in Ottawa. (He would have quickly dismissed such prideful ideas from his mind as unworthy.) And there was the growing realization that, aside from Phyllis and her boys, their four other children were busy back in Canada raising their growing families. George and Jessie yearned to be present as their grandchildren grew up. In many ways, therefore, George came to understand that in a fundamental way, and for the remainder of his life, his place was in Canada.

Accordingly, already in 1936, he and Jessie started to consider the prospects of a return to Ottawa. Then they made their decision. George did not openly discuss all these issues, and the reason he gave everyone was the financial burden of staying where they were.

By June of 1937, GPW had arranged to take up a position as a clergyman in Ottawa. After four years in England, on August 8, he and

Jessie said goodbye to this chapter of their lives as they set sail from Southampton. They arrived in Montreal on August 16, welcomed by their son Philip. Within a couple of weeks, they had moved back to Ottawa and G. P. Woollcombe began the final part of his life story.

Adventure at sea

[At this point, for the sake of continuity in the logical flow of this narrative, before describing Woollcombe's remaining time in Ottawa we will jump ahead a couple of years to recount a dramatic adventure he experienced on the high seas.]

By the summer of 1939, England was fearfully anticipating the imminent breakout of a new war with Germany. The anxiety was intense. Regardless, G. P. Woollcombe was not about to interrupt his habit of visiting his Mother Country in the summer. On the contrary, he was even more determined to be with his sisters and his brother in face of "the gathering storm" (as Churchill later described it.). In early August Hitler was amassing his troops along the Polish border ready to invade that country. Day by day, the British were feverishly preparing for war. Realizing the urgency, Woollcombe wasted no time in booking his return passage. There were thousands wanting to leave England.

His ship, the *SS Athenia*, of the Donaldson Line, regularly plied the trans-Atlantic route. She set sail from Glasgow on September 1st, the very day Germany invaded Poland. The next day she stopped in Liverpool to pick up more passengers. The ship was overcrowded: All told, there were 1103 passengers on board. They were mainly North Americans as well as some 500 desperate Jewish refugees. There were 315 crew. The ship departed Liverpool, bound for Montreal, at 4 p.m. on September 2nd. The passengers were relieved that they had escaped Europe in the nick of time.

Woollcombe had boarded the *Athenia* in Liverpool about 1 p.m. He quickly settled down to his customary routine of just another ocean voyage. As noted in his subsequent written personal account (from which are drawn many of these details), his cabin on A-deck was "very comfortable". He looked forward to congenial company since he was sharing the cabin with a young Englishman, an Anglican priest just appointed as a curate to a church in Montreal. The young man joined him for supper at the cabin-class sitting. Woollcombe then retired early and slept peacefully, as the ship cruised westwards along the south coast of Ireland.

The next day, Sunday, September 3rd, Woollcombe went down to the chapel at 7:30 a.m. to celebrate Holy Communion. For this voyage he was the ship's chaplain, appointed by the well-established missionary body, the S.P.C.K. (Society for Promoting Christian Knowledge.) Then at 10:30 a.m. he took the regular Morning Prayer service. His scripture text, from the 93rd Psalm, was aptly chosen:

> The waves of the sea are mighty, and wage furiously,
> But God, who dwelleth on high, is mightier.

In the meantime, back in England, at nine in the morning the British government had given Hitler an ultimatum, a deadline of 11:00 a.m. to announce he was withdrawing his troops from Poland. Failing this, a state of war would exist between Britain and Germany. At 11:15 a.m. Neville Chamberlain announced on BBC Radio that Britain and Germany were at war.

By noon, everyone on board the *Athenia* had seen the posted bulletin or heard the dramatic, but fully expected, news. In the afternoon, the crew boarded up the windows and painted the portholes black, in order to avoid detection from German submarines. The lifeboats were all uncovered and swung into position from which they could easily be launched. The passengers were told around which lifeboat they should assemble, in the unlikely event that should be necessary.

However, no one on the ship was worrying very much. All these measures were merely precautionary, so it was felt. There was no real danger to be feared. The ship was a passenger vessel and thus protected by international law. She was carrying no contraband cargo, and in any event she was sailing away from, not towards, Europe so there would be no purpose in a German submarine attack. Moreover, there were more than 300 U.S. citizens on board, and it was well known that Hitler did not wish to provoke the Americans. So Woollcombe was carefree, and he continued with his normal shipboard life. He had even arranged to take a short Evening Prayer service, planned for 8:30 p.m.

At 7:15 p.m. he left his cabin to go to supper, and went down the three flights of stairs to the dining-room on D-deck. Just before that, inexplicably, he had taken some money, a few £1 treasury notes and a Canadian $10 bill, from his cash-box. As he later explained, he was not apprehensive, for otherwise he might more usefully have changed his clothes; he simply felt that some higher Power had given him this guidance. The *Athenia* by now was cruising on a northwest course about 200 nautical miles (370 kms) from the northern tip of Ireland.

SS Athenia, slowly sinking, September 3, 1939.

It was 7:35 p.m. when the torpedo struck the port side of the ship and exploded in the engine room. Woollcombe had just finished his meat course. Suddenly a deafening bang filled the room! All the lights instantly went out and the whole ship trembled and lurched to port. Everything, plates and glasses and food, fell off the tables. Most of the diners were thrown to the floor amidst broken glass, chinaware, meat and potatoes. They had difficulty getting to their feet owing to the tilt of the ship. Women screamed and prayed.

Someone struck a match, and Woollcombe could see the location of the stairway. With all the others trying to do the same, he groped his way up the stairs to his cabin. There he found his flashlight but quickly gave it to a stewardess to help others in the dark. He put on his overcoat and hat, and in the dim twilight made his way to the upper deck. He quickly found lifeboat No. 4, to which he had been assigned. The killer U-Boat was actually on the surface at that point and could be seen from the *Athenia's* deck.

German submarine U-30.

The procedure for boarding the lifeboat, now suspended over the deck, and then launching it, was challenging. The women and children managed to climb aboard first with help from the men, followed, according to another survivor's report, by a few panicking Central European and White Russian refugees. Woollcombe was asked to get into the lifeboat and lie down on the floor with the others. All told, there were some 80 persons in the boat even though its capacity was supposed to be 62. Slowly the loaded boat was lowered down. There was a near spill as one of the rope pulleys malfunctioned, but then the boat settled safely on the water's surface. With several of the stronger men volunteering to row, and then pulling on the oars for all they were worth, they successfully moved the boat away from the sinking *Athenia*. Although 72 years of age and the oldest in his boat, Woollcombe did not hesitate to take his turn at the oars. The sea was rough and the boat pitched and tossed about. Many, especially the women, were seasick. Woollcombe gave his overcoat to a poor lady who was only wearing her nightgown and a scarf.

And so it went on for several hours through the night. Finally, around 3 a.m. they saw the lights of a ship. The *Athenia* took nearly ten hours before sinking and the wireless operator had sent out distress signals to which several ships responded. The lifeboats in the vicinity sent up flares to show where they were, and the rescue operation began. This was perilous and exhausting for Woollcombe and the others in the lifeboats. They first had to row their lifeboat up to one of the ships in the dark and turbulent waters, then try to manoeuver it alongside the ship, so they could climb up rope ladders. One boat got caught in the ship's propellers and 50 lives were lost. Finally, by about 5 a.m. one by one they had all been hauled aboard a large Swedish yacht, the *Southern Cross*. Once safely on board, as Woollcombe recounted, "One of the officers, seeing that I was 'all in' took me to his own cabin, gave me a stiff 'tot' of gin, and made me lie down in his own bunk."

Two hours later some 200 of those who had been rescued, including Woollcombe, opted to transfer to an American cargo ship, the *City of Flint*. Unlike the other rescue ships, she was continuing her voyage westward across the Atlantic. After this complex transfer of survivors had been completed, for nine days the American captain and his crew did all they could to accommodate their 'refugees' with food rations and makeshift 'dormitories'. They were hardly comfortable, and many were sick or injured, but they were all full of gratitude. Still many were beset with fears of their nightmare recurring. The terror of that horrendous, crashing bang of the torpedo explosion constantly returned to their minds. Every evening Rev. Woollcombe would visit them in the 'dormitories' before they retired and offered prayers for their protection from further peril during the night.

Survivors being rescued by the City of Flint.

Finally, on September 13th the *City of Flint* arrived in Halifax harbour and docked at the famous Pier 21. The rescued passengers were welcomed by a large crowd of anxious loved ones and curious spectators, a squad of doctors and nurses, and many journalists and news photographers.

The sinking of the *Athenia* by the Germans on September 3rd had instantly made major headlines in newspapers across Canada, England and the U.S.A. It was one of the first big stories as the war in Europe began. In Canada the story served to reinforce the unhesitating support most Canadians gave their government's own declaration of war on September 10th. It set the tone for media coverage of the rest of the war. This unprovoked attack on an unarmed civilian passenger ship, killing 118, was seen by all as a heinous war crime, "typical of the Huns".

The German side of this story only became known to the world in January 1946. It was at the post-war Nuremburg Trials that all the facts were revealed. At that time, it became clear that the attack was a horrible mistake. Completely inexcusable, but still a mistake. The German submarine U-30 had been on patrol northwest of Ireland. The captain, Oberleutenant Fritz-Julius Lemp had sighted the *Athenia* at 4:30 p.m. on September 3rd and submerged his sub to get a closer look through the periscope. He saw that the ship's windows and portholes were blacked out and, he mistakenly thought, she seemed to be zigzagging. He concluded she was either a troopship or an armed merchant carrier. That, he thought, made her a legitimate target according to accepted international rules of war. So he tracked the liner for three hours, until he was in the right position. Then he fired the torpedoes to sink the ship. Within minutes, his wireless operator rushed up to him with an intercepted wireless message from the *Athenia*. It was the stricken ship's distress signal. Panic-stricken at what the consequences would be for him, Lemp decided to slink away quietly and not report his mistake.

The Berlin high command first learned of the sinking from international news reports. They checked and realized it could only have been U-30. Hitler himself ordered a cover-up. He feared a repetition of the furor caused in World War I by the sinking of the passenger liner *Lusitania* in 1915 (which helped influence the U.S. to come into World War I against Germany). So Lemp was not court-martialled or even publicly blamed. Instead Goebbels spread the fantasy that the British themselves had torpedoed the *Athenia*, in an effort to enrage the U.S. and bring them more quickly into the war. (There were over 300 Americans on board.) Some anti-war American politicians actually bought this line.

The *Athenia* was the first ship sunk by the Germans in World War II. Its torpedo became, unintentionally, the first shot in the Battle of the Atlantic.

Meanwhile, after arriving in Halifax, most of the rescued passengers were put on the train to Montreal or to one of the U.S. cities. G. P. Woollcombe, however, was met by his son Edward and stayed on in Halifax with Edward's family for a couple of days, resting and regaining his strength. He then moved on to Montreal, staying overnight with the Philip Woollcombes, and finally returned back to the grateful, waiting arms of Jessie in Ottawa. Not surprisingly, this was his last trans-Atlantic crossing until 1946 when the war was over.

His last years

GPW in Ottawa in his 70s

The last period in the life of George Penrose Woollcombe was without major new departures, abrupt changes in life-style, or (except for the Athenia adventure) any great excitement. By and large, he had achieved his goals, satisfied his idealistic ambitions and ensured clear understanding of his values in the minds of those living around him. He also could look happily, indeed proudly, on his family, his children and grandchildren. He was deeply grateful for the constant, sustaining love of Jessie.

The rest of his life, from his return to Canada in 1937 until his death in 1951 were years of consolidation of the three great, lasting and interrelated purposes of his life: education, religion, and family. They were also years of continued slowing down. Gone was his driving energy that had fuelled his determined single-minded pursuit of high-minded ambition.

The first practical task confronting Jessie and George on arrival back in Ottawa was finding a place to live. Since this was a practical, domestic sort of job, it fell more to Jessie than to George, preoccupied as he was with ensuring and defining his work outside the home. They succeeded in finding a home suitable for them as well as for their daughter Phyllis and her sons. Sandy Hill seemed appropriate. It was an established, respectable, residential area, with many old and substantial family homes (most of which are still there today.) Several of the Woollcombes' friends from his Ashbury years were in this neighbourhood. House prices were affordable, this still being in the midst of the Depression. Moreover, as we shall see, it was just a few blocks from the site of GPW's new job.

So in September 1937, they purchased and settled into a fine, old, narrow, three-storey red-brick townhouse at 194 Cobourg Street. Of historical interest, their building was almost contiguous to the townhouse on Daly Avenue where GPW had lived many years previously with his first wife, Julia, and where Philip, the first Woollcombe child, had been born.

**194 Cobourg Street. This is where GPW
spent the last 14 years of his life.**

The household arrangements fell into place quite naturally. George and Jessie had their bedroom at the top of the staircase, with George's study next to it, facing the street. Phyllis and the two boys were on the upper storey. The boys, Kenneth, 11, and John, 8, entered Ashbury as day-boys, which unlike their boarding school in England, was affordable.

Phyllis, then an attractive widow of 39 years, took charge of most of the domestic chores. Over the years she cooked meals for everyone, including other family members and friends whose visits were frequent.

In 1943, six years after George and Jessie settled into their Cobourg Street home, their youngest son and his family had to move to Ottawa: George A. Woollcombe, a Lieutenant Commander in the Navy, had been assigned to Naval Headquarters, following sea-duty in the Battle of the Atlantic. In a letter, Jessie persuaded him to take a house on Besserer Street, just one block away. This further consolidated the extended family.

For long years afterwards, the grandchildren shared cheerful, sometimes irreverent memories with each other: Every Sunday after church there was dinner with roast beef and Yorkshire pudding. The family could begin eating only after Granddad had said grace, seated of course at the head of the table in his chair, which, unlike the other dining-room chairs, had arm-rests. One time after intoning "For what we are about to receive, may the Lord make us truly thankful. Amen", he immediately sternly reproached his daughter: "Phyllis, you know I don't like carrots cooked this way!" Once, when one of our older cousins complained that his egg seemed bad, Granddad assured him that "No, that's the freshness you are smelling!" We noticed how he really enjoyed his "small whisky" in the evening, and learned that Dr. Whitley, our family doctor, had given him a medical prescription for it during the post-war rationing. And then there was the time he told us he was going out to get a haircut. We giggled since we couldn't see any hair to cut!

(After GPW died in 1951, Phyllis inherited ownership of the house and stayed on there for many years, taking in long-term boarders, or "paying guests" as she called them. Thus for several decades Woollcombe family members and friends continued to visit the Cobourg Street house.)

Professionally, G. P. Woollcombe did not retire on his return to Canada. At the age of seventy, he took on a new job. It was his old vocation, an Anglican clergyman, but a new assignment and one for which he was well qualified. Several months before leaving England he had made his plans. He wrote to an old colleague, Rev. C. G. Hepburn, rector of All Saints' Church in Sandy Hill. He explained the reasons for his imminent return to Ottawa and asked if he would be accepted as assistant rector, a post currently vacant. This would be a busy full-time position in one of Ottawa's important parishes, at a time when the Anglican Church was still in its heyday. The salary would be modest but just adequate to supplement his Ashbury pension that had been abruptly and painfully cut in half the previous year.

All Saints' Church, on Laurier Avenue East, where GPW served as an Anglican clergyman, from 1908 to 1913, and from 1937 to 1951.

He had already had a long and close association with All Saints'. He had served there as curate many years previously when Ashbury was still on Argyle Avenue. In 1920, he had arranged for his chaplain at the school, Rev. Ernest Voorhis to become Hepburn's curate. And since this church was built in 1900, many of the school's prominent supporters were also All Saints' parishioners, especially those who lived in Sandy Hill. Not surprisingly, Hepburn was only too pleased with this proposal. Woollcombe then wrote to the Archbishop of Ottawa, the Most Rev. J. C. Roper, seeking his permission. Roper responded with "a general licence to officiate in the Diocese...Licence to date from Oct. 1, 1937." He confirmed Woollcombe would regain his senior position in the ecclesiastical pecking order, based on the date of his ordination 35 years previously, and ended his letter "with a very hearty personal welcome back to live and work amongst us." Once Woollcombe had settled his family into their new home, he started work right away. On Sunday, October 3rd he took his first service, Evening Prayer. Thus began the last chapter of his professional life.

From then on, year after year, he fulfilled his vocation as an active clergyman. He officiated and preached every Sunday at All Saints' either in the morning or the evening, forming a team with Hepburn. Woollcombe's sermons were known for their dignity, orthodoxy and their moral message. Many years later, one parishioner, in the published history of All Saints', recalled "the profoundly beautiful and deeply moving way in which he conducted the ceremony of Holy Communion". He often was called upon to officiate at weddings and, more frequently, at funerals. These funerals were poignant moments for Woollcombe: so many of his old friends and close associates from Ashbury years were passing away. More cheerfully, this lifelong teacher of young people would inevitably be asked to take "confirmation" classes, which at that time was a significant step in the religious education of Anglican children.

However, according to this same parish history, it was for his pastoral work – his visits to the sick and suffering in their homes or in hospital, for example – that Woollcombe was remembered with most affection and gratitude. I, the author of this biography, vividly recall that as a lad of nine or ten years my grandfather would ask me on a winter's day to be with him on these visits. I would follow him along the snowy sidewalks of Sandy Hill, towing my little sled. On the sled was packed his chalice and other equipment needed to administer the Holy Sacrament.

From the mid 1940s the aging process began to take its toll. George and Jessie Woollcombe, so active and dynamic throughout their lives, had to face the inexorable consequences of senescence. First it was Jessie. She became continually ill in 1944, and was bedridden at 194 Cobourg for much of the time. It will be remembered that she was two years older than her husband.

Jessie Mickle Woollcombe in her old age.

In the summer of 1945 everyone on both sides of the Atlantic was swept up in the euphoria unleashed by the end of the War. The Woollcombe family's joy in that historic moment was mitigated: George A. Woollcombe's stepson, Lt. John Smart, RCNVR, was lost at sea, a victim of a German U-boat attack just three weeks before Victory-in-Europe Day.

As the post-war months passed, Jessie's steady decline was of great concern. By the spring of 1946 George, on the advice of the family doctor, Harry Whitley, hired a Practical Nurse, Miss Nellie Cooksley, to live with them and attend full time to Mrs. Woollcombe.

George, too, was ill more frequently. On top of the natural ravages of aging, he was weighed down by his concerns about Jessie and by financial difficulties. In October 1946, Dr. Whitley urged him to reduce his workload at All Saints'. In January 1947 he so informed Rev. Hepburn and resigned as assistant rector. He did agree to continue assisting Hepburn with Sunday services as "Honorary Assistant".

Immediately following his resignation, Woollcombe was awarded a noteworthy distinction by the Anglican Church. On February 26, 1947 the Bishop of Ottawa appointed him honorary Canon of Christ Church Cathedral, citing his outstanding contribution in the field of education and his valuable service to the Church. From that day on, and indeed long after his death four years later, he was referred to as "Canon Woollcombe". This was the last significant honour he would receive.

It is interesting to recall at this point how the public persona of G. P. Woollcombe evolved. Consider the progression of his various ecclesiastical titles and academic awards through his lifetime. He always ensured these honours were recognized publicly. When he first arrived in Canada to teach school, he was simply "Mr. Woollcombe, B.A." or as the occasion might demand, "...B.A. (Oxon)". As soon as he was ordained deacon in 1902, and then priest in 1903, he was "Reverend" or simply "Rev.". In 1906 he could add "M.A.", or "M.A. (Oxon)". Then with McGill's honorary doctorate in 1926, for most people he became "Dr. Woollcombe". Now most impressively he could be "The Reverend Canon Dr. G. P. Woollcombe, M.A. (Oxon), LL.D."... although in fairness to his reputation, he was never known to string all these together.

Throughout these later years, G. P. Woollcombe remained closely connected with Ashbury as the revered elder statesman. Now an old man, frail and walking with a cane but always upright in bearing, he was a familiar figure on the campus. Successive headmasters (there were four successors before he died) would seek his counsel.

He remained officially on the board of governors and attended meetings whenever he could. He would frequently visit his old school to watch school sporting events or participate in services in the chapel. Sometimes he would just meet and chat with the school boys. His passion to connect with the students was never diminished. Every year he would address the assembled school, usually review Ashbury's history, always offer some advice on values and the lessons of life, and invariably request the headmaster to declare a half-holiday. At this, someone would ritualistically shout "Three cheers for the Founder!", and the chorus of boys' voices would respond: "Hip-hip-hurray" (x3), always followed, for some odd reason, by: "Tiger!"

Woollcombe would have utterly abhorred any open discussion or complaining about his financial situation. However, in 1945 and 1946 he was beset by serious anxieties. He had additional payments for Jessie's care, especially for the nurse. Miss Cooksley's wage at $100 each month was a heavy drain on his budget. At one point, his children joined together to volunteer some financial support. When his declining health forced him to retire from All Saints', that small revenue from the church was no longer there.

The Ashbury board had refused to restore the modest pension (which they called a "retaining fee") for their founder and headmaster for 42 years. As previously noted, it was cut in half in 1936 due to the school's dire financial straits. Courteously and discreetly, but to no avail, Woollcombe had repeatedly raised the matter in personal letters with the board chairman. These are still on file. He pointed out that, approaching 80 years of age, he had "necessarily very few years to live in which to burden the school". In January 1947 when his All Saints' revenue stopped, the board finally relented somewhat and raised the pension by $500, from $1500 annually to $2000. The whole affair must have been deeply humiliating for this modest but proud man, striving to focus on higher matters.

After the war, Woollcombe felt compelled to resume his visits to England. In early summer 1946, he visited his brother John and his three sisters, whom he had not seen since 1939. John's son Philip, who still is living in England, recalls details about this visit: John Woollcombe was alarmed that the only passage available for his older brother was a cargo ship, but Philip's "Uncle George" did bring humbug candies and paperback novels from Canada to console his relatives suffering from the post-war rationing.

On return to Canada that year GPW joined Jessie, staying with their son George and daughter-in-law Dorothy at a large rented cottage on Kingsmere Lake. Jessie, now in palliative care, was attended to by Miss Cooksley. The lengthy, painful vigil continued through the winter and the following summer. Jessie finally had to be moved to the Civic Hospital. She died there on July 31st 1947. Her husband's cathartic grieving could now begin.

GPW reading in his study in his last years.

Albeit slowly, Woollcombe was more or less able to continue with his regular life for the next four years. He kept up his frequent visits and other connections with Ashbury. He loved the Old Boys' reunions and made sure he was invited to their dinners. As a well-known and respected retired clergyman, he was often asked to assist at church services. He regularly visited and was visited by his children and their families. In the summers he often stayed with friends or family at their cottages.

In early March 1950, he was struck by further tragedy: his son Edward, the prominent engineer in Halifax, only 48 years old with a wife and two children, died suddenly of a heart attack. Edward's body was transported to Ottawa for the funeral and interment.

Later in 1950 GPW actually did go back to England once again, for nearly two months in June and July. There he saw his English relatives for the last time, as it turned out. Before his journey home, he proudly declared to a Reuters journalist in the lobby of his hotel that this voyage would be his 89th Atlantic crossing.

He did not intend it to be his last. On March 10th, 1951 he wrote to his son Philip:

> As I think I have intimated to you, I have decided _not_ to cross the Atlantic this summer…and then, if I am still alive and in good shape, to go back to England for a couple of months in the early summer of _1952_. *

* Underlining by GPW

This, of course, was not to be.

In the autumn of 1950, Ashbury commissioned Ottawa artist and former Ashburian, Robert Hyndman, to paint a portrait of the Founder. This nearly life-sized oil painting was formally unveiled in a ceremony on November 11. The painting still hangs prominently near the entrance to the chapel. It portrays a physically frail old man – hardly the vigorous, determined leader who created and guided Ashbury for so long. Nonetheless his strength of character clearly shines through in the portrait.

Unveiling his portrait at Ashbury, November 11, 1950. Surrounding
GPW from left to right in the photo: Robert Craig, President
of the Montreal Branch of the Old Boys' Association, GPW's
son George A. Woollcombe, his grandson Stephen Woollcombe,
E. N. Rhodes Sr. at that time Deputy Chair of the Board of
Governors, and the incumbent headmaster, R. H. Perry.

GPW's death was sudden. The summer of 1951 began in a normal fashion. In May he spent three weeks in Toronto staying with his daughter Maithol and her husband Steve Brodie. He was there to celebrate his 84th birthday on May 21st. Later followed a short visit to friends in Morrisburg and a few days with son George and family at their Meech Lake cottage. Then on Saturday, June 30 back home at 194 Cobourg with Phyllis, he complained of chest pains. She called Dr. Whitley and on Sunday an ambulance took him to the Ottawa Civic Hospital. He suffered a heart seizure there and died about 3 p.m. on Monday, July 2nd.

His funeral at All Saints' on Wednesday afternoon was attended by hundreds. Many were old Ashburians or otherwise connected with the school. Anglican Church people of course were out in force. The service was conducted by Archdeacon Hepburn. The Rt. Rev. Robert Jefferson, Bishop of Ottawa, gave the eulogy. He touched briefly on Dr. Woollcombe's career focussing on his work as one of Canada's outstanding educationalists who "trained his boys through religion, scholarship and games. He believed that a complete education is one that fitted a man to perform all offices both public and private in peace and in war". As reported in the *Ottawa Citizen*,

> *In an impressive ceremony following the service, 13 members of the local Anglican clergy formed a clerical guard of honor as the body of Canon Woollcombe was borne from the church to the hearse. At this point the carillon bells of All Saints pealed in requiem.*

George Penrose Woollcombe was then buried in the Beechwood Cemetery. It was the same family plot that he had purchased in 1898 on the death of his first wife Julia. His second wife Jessie and several others of his family rest there with him.

The Woollcombe tombstone.

Descendants of G.P. Woollcombe

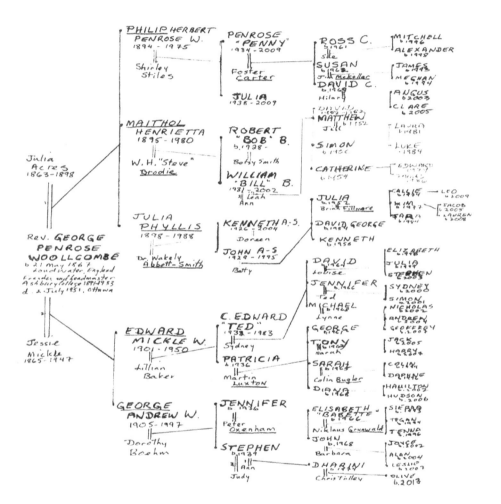

Epilogue

We have now heard the full story of George Penrose Woollcombe. We have followed his life in great detail over his 84 years. So how can we sum it all up in a few words? Who, in essence, was this man? What value did his life leave for us? What was his legacy? Why should we be interested in his story? How does it relate to our own history? Our own present concerns?

G. P. Woollcombe was first and foremost an educator. He was an Englishman who spent his working life in Canada giving Canadian boys an education. But he was also a visionary. With amazing determination, energy and total commitment, he created, and built up over four decades an outstanding Canadian school that, since 1891, has formed thousands of young Canadians.

At the core of his philosophy and his character, he was a man of God. His central values flowed therefrom. He was a clergyman as well as a schoolmaster. These were his two life professions, and they perfectly complemented each other. Just as much, he was a family man, a caring and constant son, brother, husband, father, and grandfather, a revered family patriarch.

He was a Victorian, middle-class, Church-of-Englander, educated at an English grammar school and at Oxford. As such, he was naturally conservative in his social and intellectual outlook, including in his approach to education. Such conservatism was the dominant attitude of Ottawa society of the times. However, the class consciousness and class snobbery he may have internalized by osmosis during his English education was moderated and subdued by his more egalitarian Canadian environment.

He was entirely English, but equally entirely Canadian. This paradox reflects that period of Canadian history which he occupied. Understanding Woollcombe's story gives us insight into the history of modern Canada. Canada, in part, was an organic outgrowth of Victorian England. Woollcombe was a small but integral part of this growth. The narrative of his life story paralleled Canadian history. He was born in the year of Confederation. He came to Canada in the hey-day of British imperialism. In 1891 he founded Ashbury, across from the Parliament Buildings, at the very end of Sir John A. Macdonald's regime, with the Laurier era about to begin. Ashbury's most important patrons were lumber barons, the primary industrialists of the Ottawa Valley, and indeed of Canada. His school flourished and grew during the Laurier years, a part of the growth of Ottawa and of Canada. The British con- nection in Canada, including English Canadian loyalty to the British monarch, was as strong as ever in the early 20th century, notably during "The Great War" of 1914-18. This served to sustain the popularity and the English flavour of Ashbury and of its English headmaster, right up to his retirement in 1933. In this sense, Woollcombe was a man of his times. About this time however Canada, and Ashbury as well, started distinctly to loosen the British connection and broaden its social horizons.

Without any doubt, his one great concrete legacy was Ashbury College. Under his leadership, this school became one of Canada's outstanding educational institutions. It is still that today since it has grown and flourished, and changed with the times. But Woollcombe's school was the solid historical base. Beyond its fine physical building in Rockcliffe and its high educational standards, he gave Ashbury stu- dents their backbone of values, boiled down in his own words: **to serve others, and to do your best.**

Afterword

by Norman Southward, Head of School, Ashbury College

Reaching back in one's past can be a complex task whether as an individual, a family, or an institution. However, the Woollcombe biography manages to give us unique insight into a young man of his time, his family and the early foundation of Ashbury College. It also takes us to the intersection of Woollcombe's life with a newly evolving capital city and a dominion moving towards nationhood. What started as a day school for sons of local captains of industry, has emerged as an internationally renowned day and boarding school for both boys and girls from diverse backgrounds.

"Mr. Woollcombe's School", opened with just 17 students in 1891, and now, in Ashbury's 125th year 700 students benefit from an education that holds true to many of the values that he identified.

Although much has changed since those Victorian times of the late 19th century, there are still elements of both pedagogy and program from Woollcombe's school that are central to the Ashbury of today. Our mission "to engage students in a dynamic learning environment and inspire them to become intellectually curious, compassionate and responsible citizens" finds much of its origin in the Woollcombe vision. A balanced and rigorous academic program endures as the core feature to the student experience, but where learning does not stop at the classroom door. Students continue to extend themselves in sport, the arts and service to the community. Our outlook has shifted to an even wider view of the world where students develop a truly global perspective. As Ottawa and Canada have moved beyond a demographic of "two founding nations" Ashbury is now a school enriched by the diversity of over 50 nationalities amongst its students. In many ways Ashbury is no longer a school rooted in empire, but internationally oriented in the broadest sense.

From its beginning, Ashbury developed a culture of innovation and adaptation, redefining what schooling might look like. Much has transpired since the 42-year headship of Woollcombe, and many have built on his legacy over the years. Beyond the beauty of the red brick entrance to our Rockcliffe campus, Ashbury's facilities' development is driven by program improvement and excellence. As an early IB World School, adopter of new technologies and a place where students thrive in a range of co-curricular activities from athletics to the creative arts – Ashbury seeks to build on programs of rigour and relevancy for students of the future. Moreover, Ashbury is a community that fosters kindness and compassion where one's character transcends all as students take flight in their university studies and become contributors to their communities around the world.

We are grateful for the lens that Stephen Woollcombe has provided us on the personal history of Ashbury's founder in this special 125th year. The personal link from grandfather to grandson is unique and has brought us closer to our increasingly distant past. Many individuals and their families have contributed to the school we are today, and G. P. Woollcombe's legacy, one that stands out in Canadian education, will continue to provide exceptional educational opportunities to many future Ashburians.

Acknowledgements and Sources

As I researched this book, I drew on personal memories, on family lore, old family documents and photos, and conversations with all persons who had any memories, or even second-hand recollections of G. P. Woollcombe. The various and distinct parts of GPW's life each entailed the scouring of different sources of information.

The Internet was a major source throughout, often of course starting with Google. I reviewed scores of old newspaper clippings, frequently accessed through the website Newspapers.com. Social notices in *The Ottawa Journal* often informed me about GPW's comings and goings and his transatlantic travel dates were sometimes confirmed by ships' passenger lists, available on line. Census information was similarly accessible.

In delving into GPW's origins and early life in England, my main sources were old family papers, the passed-on childhood recollections of his only surviving nephew, Philip Woollcombe who lives in England, Google Maps and various websites, including that of the Royal Grammar School, High Wycombe.

On the Oxford years, beyond GPW's papers, I received pertinent advice from the Archivist of Christ Church, Judith Curthoys and her colleagues, who were able to search for GPW's records. On her advice I surveyed and drew from several historical books, notably:

- *The History of the University of Oxford*, eds. M.G.Brock and M.C.Curthoys, Volume VII: Nineteenth-Century Oxford, Part 2; Clarendon Press, Oxford, 1997.

- Dacre Balsdon, *Oxford Now and Then*, Duckworth, London, 1970.

- Judith Curthoys, *The Cardinal's College: Christ Church, Chapter and Verse*, Profile Books Ltd., London, 2012.

- *Oxford Men 1880 – 1892*, ed. Joseph Foster, Oxford, 1893
- as well as the websites of Christ Church and of Oxford University.

Concerning GPW's connections with Bishop's College, and Bishop's College School, Lennoxville, I was helped by correspondence with the University Archivist, Anna M. Grant, and by reading the history of BCS by J. Graham Patriquin, *From Little Forks to Moulton Hill*, BCS, Lennoxville, 1978.

On Canada and Ottawa in the late 19th and early 20th centuries my sources, too numerous to list, include books, articles, historical plaques on buildings and browsing in the Ottawa Public Library, City of Ottawa Archives, Library and Archives Canada, Carleton University library, and the Bytown Museum. Several books gave flavour and specifics. They include: Sandra Gwyn *The Private Capital: Ambition and Love in the Age of Macdonald and Laurier*, McLelland & Stewart, Toronto, 1984; Richard Gwyn, *Nation Maker: Sir John A. Macdonald: His Life, Our Times*, Random House, Toronto, 2011; Naomi Slater Heydon *Looking Back…Pioneers of Bytown and March*, M.O.M. Printing, Ottawa,

On GPW's life as a clergyman and his relationship with the Anglican church in Ottawa, much information came from old newspaper clippings. However, I fruitfully searched the files in the archives of the Diocese of Ottawa, assisted by Glenn Lockwood, Archivist and Registrar. GPW served many years at All Saints' Church, Sandy Hill. The history of this church entitled *The First Ninety Years*, a 1989 monograph by C. H. Little, was useful.

Information about GPW's return to England in 1933 and his years there until 1937 as Vicar of Woodford Halse is drawn from his correspondence and photos on file, from family memories, and from the Internet, in particular the website of Woodford Halse, and Google Maps. The story of the sinking of the *SS Athenia* in September 1939 was helpfully recorded by two detailed reports of the adventure, one by GPW himself and the other by a fellow survivor. The Internet provided much of the historical context, as well as three photos of the sinking, which have been released by the Imperial War Museum for non-commercial use.

The support of Ashbury College for writing and publishing this book has been critical. For this I wish to thank the Head of School, Norman Southward, who has done everything to make this project a success. Woollcombe was Head #1 of Ashbury; Southward is Head #10. The responsibility for the content in this book is entirely my own and I have been fully independent of any control by the school. However, Norman's enthusiastic encouragement, practical support and wise advice have been precious to me. I also thank him for his 'Afterword' which relates Ashbury's past to its present.

Of course the major part of my research for this book related to GPW's work and life with Ashbury, starting at the school's very beginning in 1891. The school College archives were my principal source in this regard, notably GPW's correspondence, minutes of Board meetings, and old issues of the school magazine, *The Ashburian*. Of great help has been Victoria Wilgress, Ashbury Relations Ambassador who is in charge of the archives. From the beginning Vicky has been constantly supportive of this GPWbio project.

A critically important source book was the history of the school published to celebrate the school's centennial, by Tony German, *A Character of its Own: Ashbury College 1891 – 1991*, Creative Bound Inc., Carp, Ontario. Even more directly helpful was the research on file in the archives done to prepare background for Tony German's book. Much of this research was the work of Andrew M. Johnston who at the time was studying history at the University of Toronto. He had graduated from Ashbury in 1983 and now is a history professor at Carleton University. Andrew has been a helpful source of advice to me.

Tara Jackson, Director of Communications and Marketing at Ashbury has effectively arranged for the contract with my publishers, FriesenPress.

The book has 61 photographs throughout. Many are old snapshots and portraits from family files. Some are from the Ashbury archives. A few I have taken from the Internet. Four colour photos near the end of the book were taken by my friend Tom Schatzky, a highly skilled amateur photographer. Over several hours, all the photos were expertly reviewed at Ashbury and some greatly improved with Photoshop by Lisa Bettancourt, a teacher in the Arts Department and specialist in photography, assisted by talented Grade 11 student, Max Jiang. Lisa's professional skill and commitment has resulted in a better appearance for the book.

Over the past two years I have received excellent editorial advice. Retired professor at UBC and author John R. Wood, eminent Canadian historian and my neighbour Charlotte Gray, and retired World Bank economist Richard Hamilton all read over the manuscript at earlier stages and made helpful suggestions on the organization and content.

More recently. my sister-in-law Kathi Fleming McInnes, my step-daughter Sally Barber, and my friend Mary Morican all kindly volunteered to sharpen their pencils and go through the whole text correcting many scores of unnoticed spelling, grammar, punctuation mistakes, or missing or repeated words or phrases.

My sister Jennifer Woollcombe Oxenham, the only person alive who remembers GPW as well or better than I do, has been a constant, close supporter, editor and advisor on content at every stage, almost every page, of the project. Her drafting skill is only surpassed by her sharp insights.

I wish to thank Andrew Cohen, journalist and author, for writing a 'foreword' that pertinently complements and graces the biography, as well as Jean Teron and Andrew Johnston for their kind testimonials on the back cover.

My daughter Dharini, GPW's great-granddaughter, graduated from the school in 1993 and thus has carried on the centuries-old

Woollcombe-Ashbury connection. She has encouraged me all along with this book.

Finally, my wife Judy Barber Woollcombe has read through and wisely commented on various parts of the manuscript, but mainly she has been a strong source of strength for me throughout the whole project.

About The Author

Stephen Woollcombe is uniquely qualified to write the story of G.P. Woollcombe. As his grandson, he provides personal memories of the man amongst his family, friends and former students. As a researcher and historian, he has collected anecdotal and archival information that provide a comprehensive and factual narrative of an important Canadian educator, set in the context of Canadian history. The book, he notes, is "a labour of love and curiosity".

As a boy, Stephen attended Ashbury College in Ottawa, the school his grandfather founded. After university studies in Toronto and Quebec City, he followed the family calling to educate and served as a volunteer teacher in India. Subsequently, he enjoyed a long career as a Canadian diplomat, with postings in five continents. In retirement, he taught university courses in Ottawa and Venezuela, has been active in politics at the federal level and has been engaged in various social concerns in Canada and development work abroad.

Now, decades later, Stephen remains close to Ashbury College. His book's publication coincides with the school's 125th anniversary.

CPSIA information can be obtained
at www.ICGtesting.com
Printed in the USA
LVOW06s0109270816
501586LV00001B/1/P